ACTING SONGS
David Brunetti

Acting Songs

Copyright © 2006 by David Brunetti

All rights reserved. No part of the publication may be reproduced or transmitted in any form or by any means, electronic or mechanical, including photcopy, recording or any information storage and retrieval system, without permission in writing from the publisher.

Cover design, book design by Henry Beer
Rights to lyrics secured by Kevin McKiernan at Creative License

EMBRACEABLE YOU, by George Gershwin and Ira Gershwin; ©1930 (Renewed) WB Music Corp.; All Rights Reserved; Used by Permission; WARNER BROS. PUBLICATIONS U.S. INC., Miami FL. 33014

I COULD HAVE DANCED ALL NIGHT, by Alan Jay Lerner and Frederick Loewe; ©1956 (Renewed) by Alan Jay Lerner and Frederick Loewe; Chappell & Co. owner of publications and allied rights throughout the World; All Rights Reserved; Used by Permission; WARNER BROS. PUBLICATIONS U.S. INC., Miami FL. 33014

JUST IN TIME, by Betty Comden, Adolph Green, Jule Styne; ©1956 (Renewed) Stratford Music Corporation; All Rights Administered by Chappell & Co.; All Rights Reserved; Used by Permission; WARNER BROS. PUBLICATIONS U.S. INC., Miami, FL 33014

MY SHIP, by Ira Gershwin and Kurt Weill; ©1941 (Renewed) Ira Gershwin Music (ASCAP) and TRO-Hampshire House Publ. Corp.; All Rights o/b/o Ira Gershwin Music administered by WB Music Corp. (ASCAP); All Rights reserverd; Used by Permission; WARNER BROS. PUBLICATIONS U.S. INC., Miami, FL. 33014

SEND IN THE CLOWNS, by Stephen Sondheim; ©1973 Rilting Music. Inc. (ASCAP); All Rights Administered by WB Music Corp.; All Rights Reserved; Used by Permission; WARNER BROS. PUBLICATIONS U.S. INC., Miami, FL. 33014

SOMEONE TO WATCH OVER ME, by George Gershwin and Ira Gershwin; ©1926 (Renewed) WB Music Corp.; All Rights Reserved; Used by Permission; WARNER BROS. PUBLICATIONS U.S. INC., Miami, FL. 33014

BEING ALIVE, by Stephen Sondheim; ©1970 (Renewed) Range road Music Inc., Quartet Music Inc. and Rilting Music, Inc.; All Rights administered by Herald Square Music Inc.; All Rights Reserved; Used by Permission

A QUIET THING, by John Kander and Fred Ebb; ©1965, Alley Music Corp. and Trio Music Company, Inc.; Copyright renewed.; All Rights Reserved; Used by Permission

WHY DID I CHOOSE YOU?; From THE YEARLING; Lyric by Herbert Martin; Music by Michael Leonard; ©1965 (Renewed) HERBERT MARTIN and MICHAEL LEONARD; All Rights Controlled by EDWIN H. MORRIS & COMPANY, A Division of MPL Communications, Inc. and EMANUEL MUSIC CORP.; All Rights Reserved; Used by Permission

Library of Congress Control Number: 2006909485
Publisher: BookSurge, LLC, North Chareston, South Carolina
isbn # 1-4196-5198-6

This book is dedicated to the two great acting teachers
with whom I had the privilege of studying:
John Ulmer and Hal Holden.
They were brilliant, generous teachers.
I love them and I miss them.

Preface

I SET OUT TO WRITE THE BOOK I WISH HAD EXISTED when I came to New York as a young singing actor. I wanted a method of working on songs that would allow me to combine what I'd learned about truthful acting with what I knew about music. Over the years, as a performer and later as a coach, I combined what I'd learned from my teachers with some of my own ideas, and that's the process I describe in this book.

Scattered throughout the book you'll find quotes from interviews I conducted with a number of people who are prominent in the musical theater: composers, lyricists, producers, directors, choreographers, musical directors, talent agents, casting directors, a critic and a record producer. These are result-oriented people working today who make decisions about which singing actors get which jobs. They had a lot of illuminating things to say, and I hope you'll find their words as inspiring as I do.

CONTENTS

Introduction	1
The Song	5
The Monologue	10
The Rhythm	45
The Melody	50
Gestures And Focus	56
Character Acting	60
Auditions	63
Studying The Work Of Masters	77
Additional Thoughts	81
Biographies	85

Introduction

MOST OF THE ACTING WE SEE in the movies and much of the acting we see on professional stages in America is what is called Method Acting. There are a number of other words used to describe this type of performing: organic, internal, truthful, emotionally-connected, presentational. In this work, the actor has found a way to experience honest-to-God "real living within a set of imaginary circumstances." (This is a definition of good acting coined by the great and seminal American acting teacher Sanford Meisner.) Truthful actors aren't pretending to talk to each other in a scene—they really are talking to each other, using the dialogue supplied by the playwright or screenwriter. They aren't pretending to see things, hear things, touch things—they really are seeing, hearing and touching. They aren't pretending to care and to feel and to accomplish—they have found a way to actually

> I'm always looking for an honesty, a truthfulness.
> Scott Ellis, Director

> People think singing is "Oh, this is singing. It must be different." And what you want to show them is that it's not different. Singing is acting.
> David Friedman,
> Composer/Lyricist, Conductor

> When singers are not being truthful about the lyric in terms of themselves and their own psyche, they don't sing as well. You have to bring your psyche and your history and baggage to the lyric.
> Mike Berniker, Record Producer

care and feel and accomplish within the imaginary world of the play or movie.

At the other end of the spectrum is a different acting approach, which is called external, artificial, intellectual, representational. In this way of working the actors make decisions about what a character would look like and sound like if they were indeed living through the situation of the play or movie, and then they do their best to represent that on stage—to simulate external behavior. The technical term for this is "indicating." These actors are working out of their intellects, trying to make a calculated effect on the audience. They are pretending to feel, to see, to hear—pretending to live on stage, always with a part of their psyche sitting in the audience, watching and judging. Their work ultimately is emotionally-disconnected, unoriginal and uninvolving. They themselves aren't viscerally involved—how could an audience be involved? You can see external, empty actors in amateur theater productions everywhere. Without realizing there is an alternative, most untrained actors go without hesitation to this kind of performing.

Another term used to describe external acting is "technical acting." That designation always irks me. Method actors are also technical actors. First of all, any really good actor has studied and mastered external techniques—healthy, flexible use of the body and voice. But that's not nearly enough. It is also possible to develop an emotional technique, a technique that allows you to be fully, truly alive under imaginary circumstances. Children do it naturally. When kids are talking to Santa or Grandma on their toy telephones, or when they're playing house or war, they have a fantastic ability to believe in the make-believe they've set up, ("I'll be the mommy, you be the daddy...") and then to live within that make-believe with spontaneity and emotional aliveness. It's so much fun to watch children playing when they don't know they're being watched. They're alive, fresh, improvisational and unpredictable. The instant they become aware of being observed, however, things change. They become phony and self-conscious; they go "into their heads" and lose their spontaneity. Their play becomes full of clichés as they try to give a good performance to impress their audience. At first they were really living under imaginary circumstances, but then they start pretending to live, and boy is that boring.

In New York in the 1930s a group of theater artists—actors, directors and writers—joined together and put on shows. They called themselves the Group Theatre. They had been inspired by the work of artists from the Moscow Art Theatre under Constantin Stanislavsky, and they brought that work to life in America. The preeminent teachers who emerged from the Group Theatre were Lee Strasberg, Stella Adler, Harold Clurman, Bobby Lewis, and Sanford Meisner. They were passionately committed to a new way of doing things. They cared about truthful, deeply felt, human work. They knew that the truth touched people, moved people, changed people, and they created ways of teaching and working that still permeate the movies and theater produced in America today.

The best and most important work done in the musical theater incorporates this same kind of acting. There's a frequent misconception among musical theater practitioners that somehow we don't really need to act in musicals; that there's "real" acting in plays and movies and then there's "musical theater" acting; that we don't need to learn to be truthful and emotionally-connected actors; that learning to sing and dance is enough. Nothing could be further from the truth. The great performing artists of the musical theater, including Gwen Verdon, Bert Lahr, Julie Andrews, Barbara Cook, Richard Kiley, Liza Minelli, Betty Buckley, Bernadette Peters and Mandy Patinkin have all had something in common—not only have they all been accomplished to varying degrees as singers and dancers, but they've all been organic actors. They've all used their own deep, personal, idiosyncratic inner lives in their work. They're all really "method actors," and that's why people respond to them so powerfully. They reveal their deepest feelings, needs and vulnerabilities in their performances, and that's interesting. There is nothing more moving than the truth. It's compelling and ultimately a healing experience to watch performers really live on stage and screen. That's the kind of work I care about and that's the kind of work this book is aimed at generating.

The Song

Actors who aren't interested or skilled in organic acting most often do the following kind of work on a script: they sit alone and go over their lines, deciding how they should say them once they get to rehearsal. "I'll emphasize this word here, then I'll take a nice pause, then I'll say this last part very slowly, really emphasizing this word…." They say their lines out loud, trying to make them sound just right. They practice their "line readings." Method actors avoid line readings like the plague. When you read a review in which the critic admires or criticizes an actor's line readings you can bet that critic knows little about organic acting. Making intellectual decisions in advance about the way lines should be spoken is a perfect way to rob your performance of spontaneity and inner life. In American acting we respond organically and genuinely to what the other actors are "giving us" in a scene. To have already decided how a line should be said most often

> I always look for individuality and people who dance, sing and act with character. It's always about the acting. Always. I'm not impressed by empty triple turns, by empty high E's. I'm not impressed by technique. I'm just not. I will hire somebody with less technique and more emotional connection, or more individual acting sensibility in their dance or in their song. That's always more interesting and exciting to me.
>
> Rob Marshall,
> Director/Choreographer

stops you from truly living and responding from moment to moment—and an audience can sense the difference.

I knew an actress who had toured extensively with Richard Kiley in "Man of La Mancha." She played the housekeeper, one of the supporting roles. They were in the midwest, having been on tour for months. Kiley originated the role of Don Quixote on Broadway and by this time he had played it thousands of times. One evening some of the actors got silly on stage. They were fried after traveling and having played hundreds of performances, and they weren't concentrating. Something cracked them up and there they were on stage trying to stifle their giggles—not the professional behavior you'd expect in a first-class production. At that point in the show Kiley stepped on stage to deliver a monologue—one that he usually spoke loudly and robustly. But on this night he saw the other actors out there behaving like three-year-olds, and he spoke his lines very quietly and with intense concentration, drilling them into his naughty co-workers—he scared the hell out of them. He knew how to live on stage, using and responding to what was really going on, not locked into some pre-conceived pattern of line readings and behavior.

Now, having said all this about the evils of line readings, here's some startling news: *a song is a monologue with line readings.* The difference between a monologue in a play and a song in a musical is, of course, the music. The actor in a musical is not simply given the text to bring to life. He's also responsible for melody and rhythm—the words are set to music. All natural human speech contains melody and rhythm. As we speak our voices go up and down in pitch and the words come out in varied rhythms. In an effort to communicate to others what we're feeling and thinking, we choose words and vocalize them, using different pitches and rhythms to make ourselves understood. And so these elements of music—melody and rhythm—are a natural part of everyday human experience. Our speech is always musical, we're always "singing." Notes on a staff simply represent this natural phenomenon. Using a sophisticated enough system of music notation, ordinary human speech could be represented by writing notes on music paper. Our western music system is too limited to record human speech precisely, with its infinite variations of pitch and rhythm, but nonetheless, when we sing the words of a song we are really *speaking* them in pre-ordained rhythmic patterns on pre-ordained pitches. Voila—line readings!

In writing a musical, the first order of business is usually to outline the overall story structure. Then, after the individual scenes are mapped out, the writers look to find the major emotional points in the scene. Where are the big decisions made? Where are the biggest feelings or needs expressed? And those are the moments that are musicalized, made into songs or dances. The musicalized moment is the most expressive part of the scene.

It takes a tremendous amount of skill to sing a

> When I'm writing I think about the character. That's all I think about. I think about the character, the emotion in the situation. I try to imagine what the character is feeling, what the rhythms of their speech are, what the rhythms of their emotional life are. It's like I'm acting. It's "method writing." You put yourself so far in there that when you're writing, it's not like you're writing at all.
>
> *Stephen Flaherty, Composer*

> Rock singers live their songs, maybe even more than pre-rock singers, because they're not playing characters. The songs are all about themselves and their experiences.
>
> *Stephen Holden, Critic*

> Directing straight plays and musicals is basically the same experience, in that the truthfulness has to be there. You approach the work in exactly the same way as far as character development is concerned. You ask the same questions, you explore it in the same way. In a musical, that character eventually has to sing, and I approach a song as just the continuation of the scene. When I sit down with a cast to read a musical on the first day of rehearsal, I always have the actors read the lyrics just as if they are part of the script. If it's all working the song lyric should be a continuation of the scene.
>
> *Scott Ellis, Director*

song, honoring the melodies and rhythms—the line readings—and at the same time bringing the text to life: to have a human, spontaneous, emotionally-alive experience, the kind of experience that every good organic actor strives to have—to live it now. It's an advanced acting technique. It's difficult but it's possible, and it's a beautiful thing to behold when it's done by a real artist. Maria Callas could do it. Mahalia Jackson could do it. Billie Holiday, Frank Sinatra and Judy Garland could do it. Janis Joplin and Patsy Cline could do it. Mick Jagger, Bette Midler and k.d. lang can do it. And you can do it.

I propose a series of steps to be taken as you learn and rehearse a song. Work slowly. It will pay off. Don't rush into some big performance. If you do that you're bound to end up pushing and indicating—pretending to feel things you're not really feeling. Build your performance from the inside out. Don't worry about the results. Instead, involve yourself in the process. If you become accustomed to working slowly, deeply and organically, then even when you're in a situation where results are demanded quickly, such as one-week stock or a cold reading at an audition, you'll be better equipped to bring something truthful and alive to your work.

The Monologue

The first step I suggest is to work on the lyric of the song as a monologue, without any concern for the melody or rhythm. We'll add those later. It's a good idea to have someone play through the music of the song initially for you, so that you'll know the basic feel of the piece, and this, in turn, will affect the decisions you'll make along the way. But then set the music aside. Write out the lyrics as if they were simply a speech. Then proceed to get the monologue "on its feet."

Some of the songs you'll work on will be from hit musicals for which the scripts will be easily available. When that's the case, read the script and explore how the song operates within the story. It's common practice for actors working on monologues from non-musical plays to find out all they can about their characters by reading the whole play. What does your character want? How does he or

> I find it strange that a lot of performers don't look at the text as text when they're singing a song. Sometimes they won't even know what a word will mean. And I think that there are some very basic things, like making sure that you connect thoughts, even if there's a rest in the music, that you think of What is the sentence? What is the phrase? Logically, not just musically.
>
> Ted Sperling, Musical Director/Director/Orchestrator

> When you sing, yes, show your voice, but put the lyric first.
>
> Joseph Church, Musical Director/Composer

she react and behave in the circumstances of the play? How do other characters in the play feel about and act towards your character? What does the script tell you about the circumstances leading up to your monologue? What kind of economic, social, and cultural world does your character inhabit? Answering all of these questions by analyzing the whole play can help you deepen, expand and make specific the life you bring to the performance.

But very often you'll be dealing with songs from shows for which no libretto (or script, or "book") has survived. The only material available from many musicals is the songs. The good news is that well-written theater songs express a single, meaningful, human experience that an actor can understand and bring to life by studying the lyrics and music alone. In most instances you don't need access to the complete script of a musical in order to act its songs. You can act any well-written song. Many songs not written within a theatrical context are still very theatrical and therefore very actable—standards from the 1930s and 1940s written by tin-pan alley composers, songs by Billy Joel or the Beatles and so forth.

> If you're an actor/singer/dancer the most important thing is the acting. Get into acting class. Even dancers, because they should be thinking or feeling something on every move. I can tell if they're just empty. We're in the business of telling stories, and everybody is a character in that story. Even in a farce like "Little Me." You can even move me in that kind of material, if you believe it. And if you don't believe it, I don't believe it. It's that simple.
>
> *Rob Marshall,*
> *Director/Choreographer*

A. Getting To The Essence

I'll begin by analyzing a wonderful song from a musical for which the script is long lost. The musical is "The Yearling" and the song is "Why Did I Choose You?" The lyrics are by Herbert Martin and the music is by Michael Leonard. I'll look at it without any reference to its original theatrical setting. Here are the lyrics:

Why did I choose you?
What did I see in you?
I saw the heart you hide so well;
I saw a quiet man (girl)
Who had a gentle way,
A way that caught me in its glowing spell.

Why did I want you?
What could you offer me?
A love to last a lifetime through.
And when I lost my heart
So many years ago,
I lost it lovingly and willingly to you.
If I had to choose again,
I would still choose you.

A cursory hearing of the music tells us that this is a simple, lovely ballad. With that knowledge we're launched in a certain emotional direction. If the music were jagged and angry we'd have a different animal on our hands and we'd head in a different direction.

Having heard the music, we'll start digging into the text. After writing out the lyrics, read them out loud in a simple, relaxed way, just to understand their sense. Don't "act them out" or perform them in any way. Remember, work slowly.

Don't pretend to be charged up about something when you don't really have anything going on inside.

The process we're beginning now is called Preparation. Preparation is conscious, intellectual work geared towards getting you turned on emotionally within a set of imaginary circumstances. It's a conscious manipulation of the unconscious. The job of the actor is to bring the text to life—to live it with authentic emotion. Preparation gets you ready to live the text.

> It's always wonderful to hear perfect notes, but I think it's more important to see a character come alive. The essence of theater for me is when the words that you're speaking seem as if you're speaking them for the first time.
>
> Stephen Flaherty, Composer

After you've read through the lyrics ask yourself What is this song about? What's the core human experience this song deals with? As I've said, most good songs are about one thing. Boil the lyric down to a single phrase that expresses a human action. A formula that can be useful is to say:

*This song is about a person...*and choose a verb. I'd say that "Why Did I Choose You?" is about *a person reassuring someone*. Look at the Gershwin song "Embraceable You":

Embrace me,
My sweet embraceable you.
Embrace me,
You irreplaceable you.
Just one look at you—my heart grew
Tipsy in me;
You and you alone bring out the gypsy
In me.

I love all
The many charms about you;
Above all,
I want my arms about you.
Don't be a naughty baby,
Come to papa (mama)—come to papa (mama)—do!
My sweet embraceable you.

This song might be about *a person imploring someone to love them.*

"Just In Time" by Comden, Green, and Styne:

Just in time,
I found you just in time.
Before you came my time
Was running low.

I was lost,
The losing dice were tossed.
My bridges all were crossed,
Nowhere to go.

Now you're here,
And now I know just where I'm going.
No more doubt or fear,
I've found my way.

For love came just in time,
You found me just in time,
And changed my lonely life
That lovely day.

"Just In Time" might be about *a person letting someone know what a difference they've made in their life.* Other songs are more subtle and emotionally complex than these, but I still urge you to ask, What is this song about? What am I doing in this song? Get to the heart of it. Here's the lyric to "Send In the Clowns," by Stephen Sondheim:

Isn't it rich?
Are we a pair?
Me here at last on the ground,
You in mid-air.
Send in the clowns.

Isn't it bliss?
Don't you approve?
One who keeps tearing around,
One who can't move.
Where are the clowns?
Send in the clowns.

Just when I'd stopped
Opening doors,
Finally knowing
The one that I wanted was yours,
Making my entrance again
With my usual flair,
Sure of my lines, no one is there.

Don't you love farce?
My fault, I fear.
I thought that you'd want what I want—
Sorry, my dear.
But where are the clowns?
Quick, send in the clowns.
Don't bother, they're here.

> Lyrics are part of a scene. They just happen to have music to them. It's dialogue, or it's monologue. It's just set to music. It's no different. In fact as a songwriter, as a lyric writer, I usually take what the book writer has written—monologues—and just work them into a lyric, extend them into a lyric. Lyrics and scenes should be seamless; it should all be part of the same conversation. I try very hard when writing lyrics to make them sound like conversation, only heightened, a little more poetic.
>
> Lynn Ahrens, Lyricist/Librettist

This song might be about *a person letting someone know the anguish they're in*. Someone may disagree with your interpretation, but that doesn't matter—make a decision for yourself about what the song is about, and keep it short and simple.

Another way to distill the essence of a song is to imagine this: you've been rehearsing the song for a new musical, but the director tells you that the show's running too long and your song must be cut. He asks you to write a single line of dialogue to replace the song. Make it human and real, something someone might actually say. For "Why Did I Choose You?" you might come up with: "I loved you when we met, and I love you just as much now." For "Just In Time" it might be "I was in so much trouble, but you saved me." For "Send In the Clowns" it might be "Something tragic has happened here." If you have trouble understanding the central point of a song, try going to the last section of lyrics. Usually that's where the main point is made. For instance in "My Ship" by Ira Gershwin and Kurt Weill:

*My ship has sails that are made of silk—
The decks are trimmed with gold—
And of jam and spice
There's a paradise
In the hold.*

*My ship's aglow with a million pearls,
And rubies fill each bin;
The sun sits high
In a sapphire sky
When my ship comes in.*

*I can wait the years
Till it appears—
One fine day one spring.
But the pearls and such,
They won't mean much
If there's missing just one thing:*

*I do not care if that day arrives—
That dream need never be—
If the ship I sing
Doesn't also bring
My own true love to me—
If the ship I sing
Doesn't also bring
My own true love to me.*

The first half of the song talks about how splendid "my ship" will be when it comes in. It's not until the last section that we learn it's really a love song. The singer's point is that even the most glorious "ship" will mean nothing without "my own true love." We could say that "My Ship" is about *a person letting someone know that their love is by far the most important thing.*

> Well look, anybody who's any good is living their songs in some way. Julie Wilson tears them out of herself. She brings them up from the center of her life and experience in this comic and tragic way that's about as close to raw experience as you can convey by singing. Not everybody does that. Hardly anybody does that, and I don't expect everyone to do that. I expect them to have some sort of personal perspective on it, but tearing it out of your own experience, from your guts, is something that few people do. She does that.
>
> Stephen Holden, Critic

B. The Objective

Once you've come up with a succinct way of stating the song's central action, ask this: Why do I take this action? What result am I after? What do I hope will happen as a result of me singing this song? This is called the **Objective**. It's crucial that you have a job to get accomplished via the song. It's as if something is wrong in your imaginary world and singing the song will hopefully make it right. Looking again at "Why Did I Choose You?," I've suggested as the central action "to reassure." I reassure somebody so that they'll feel secure and happy, right? Finish this sentence for every song you work on:

If things go the way I want them to, after I sing this song...

For "Why Did I Choose You?" you might say "...my friend will feel secure and happy."

For "Embraceable You" you might say "...I'll get to go to bed with this person."

For "Just In Time" you might say "...my friend will

know how much they've changed my life."

For "My Ship" you might say "...my lover will believe that I value them above all else."

For "Send In the Clowns" you might say "...this person I love will change their mind and stay here with me," or perhaps "...they'll leave, but at least my dignity will be intact."

Once again, don't get hung up on coming up with the perfect objective. There is no right or wrong. Use your common sense and make the best decision you can.

> When you come in with no point of view about the song, I have learned nothing except about your technique, and when that happens I don't want you in my show. So you have a high voice—what are you going to bring to the stage? I'm looking for someone who takes me there, so I have to believe that you believe what you're singing.
>
> Rob Marshall,
> Director/Choreographer

C. The Obstacle

At this point we begin to do a little playwriting—we cook up an imaginary situation out of which the song will emerge. The situation must contain the element most central to all drama: **Conflict**. There must be an **Obstacle** in the way of you accomplishing your objective. Your goal is to create for yourself, out of your own life and imagination, a scene in which you will need to sing your song in order to resolve a conflict. As I said above, something needs to be very wrong in your imaginary world, and you come up with a way—the song—to rectify things, to change things so that they're to your liking, and if you don't achieve your objective you will suffer serious, detrimental consequences. We'll set up circumstances so that we have a goal that we're after but there's an obstacle in our way, then we'll use the song to overcome the obstacle. If I'm working on "Why Did I Choose You?" and I've decided that it's about reassuring someone, and that if I get my way, my friend will feel happy and secure after I sing to them, then I must set up a situation wherein my friend is feeling unhappy and insecure. Set up your world so that the opposite of your objective exists before you sing the song. Don't be subtle. If your objective is to get an embrace, set it up so that your imaginary partner has no intention of embracing you. If your objective is for your friend to know how much they've changed your life for the better, set it up so that they don't know that—perhaps they think you take them for granted, and it's important to you that they know the truth. If your objective is to get the person you love to stay with you by describing your painful circumstances, get the person on their way out the door, unaware of what you're going through. If your objective is to have your lover believe that they come first with you, set it up so that they're afraid other things (perhaps your career) are your first priority.

When I say "set it up," this is what I mean: Create for yourself an imaginary situation, based on your life experiences, which contains a conflict that the song can resolve. You'll need to make decisions about the following:

- Who am I talking to?
- What do I want from them?
- What obstacle is in my way?
- What happens if I don't achieve my goal?
- Where are we?
- What time is it?

You'll answer all these questions in ways that will activate you into singing the song. Remember, it's not meant to be an intellectual exercise. We're looking for ways to get ourselves going emotionally. "What situation can I come up with that will get me turned on into this song?"

Begin speaking now in the first person. Not "this is about someone trying to reassure their lover," but "this is about me trying to reassure my lover." Setting up your circumstances from the first person point of view will get you cooking right away—there's no "someone" living through this situation, there's you. Say "I" instead of "he" or "she." For an organic actor it's an important psychological device.

So, to set up a world for "Why Did I Choose You" I know that I need to be talking to someone I love profoundly, probably my "significant other," who at this moment badly

> I conducted "Song and Dance" on Broadway, with Betty Buckley, who replaced Bernadette Peters, as the star. The first act is just Betty alone on stage talking to imaginary people. And the Shuberts came in and closed the show—they surprised everyone by announcing that they were closing the show at the end of the week. Betty had just come in five weeks earlier, and thought that it would run longer, and she was shocked. So we did the show, and afterwards she said, "Was I alright in that show?" And I said, "Yes. It was different, but it was wonderful." She said, "Because every time a door opened one of the Shuberts walked in!" So in her imagination she saw them and she just played it to whoever was there. Different people walked in and she went with it.
>
> *David Friedman,*
> *Composer/Lyricist/Conductor*

needs reassurance. A less than meaningful relationship won't do—songs and plays aren't written about unimportant relationships. We need to "cast" someone in the role. It's usually not a good idea to use a current romantic relationship; it's too volatile. If you're trying to sing a warm love ballad to your spouse, but in reality you're ready to kill them after this morning's fight, you'll be out of luck. Instead, use your imagination. This is one of the great things about acting—you get to pretend to be in a relationship with anyone you choose. You can use someone in your current life, like the manager of the restaurant where you work, on whom you have a huge crush. You can use someone from your past, or you can even use someone you've never met, like a movie star who turns you on. It needs to be someone to whom you are truly, deeply attracted. Make a choice—if they're the wrong person you'll know it soon enough and you can recast them. Use people, places and things from your own life experience as you create your imaginary situation. If you grew up doing summer stock in Pittsburgh, you can use that. If you would push your grandmother down the steps for a chance to be in a new Stephen Sondheim musical, you can use that. If you had a high school teacher who believed in your talent and gave you the nurturance you didn't get at home, you can use that. If your mother died last week, do not use that. Acting can be very therapeutic but it's not therapy, and it's not safe or healthy to try to use unresolved emotional traumas that could get out of control.

Begin to "tell yourself a story" that will prepare you to bring the lyrics to life. There are clues in the lyric for what your preparation needs to include: the person you're singing to is quiet and gentle, tends to hide their feelings, their "heart." Choose someone who fits that description. Imagine a world in which you met them "so many years ago." And as we've said, they're in desperate need of reassurance. Use real elements from your own life, and then use your imagination to spin it out, like so:

"Jim and I have been together for 15 years. We met doing summer stock together in Pittsburgh and we've been together ever since. He's a big muscular guy, but he's as gentle as a lamb. I remember when we first met doing that musical review, Jim seemed to be a real loner, quiet and aloof, not close to anyone. I was very insecure about my singing back then. One evening Jim walked me out to the parking lot after I'd had a particularly depressing rehearsal, and in his soft, unassuming way he assured me that I sounded just fine, and that my strong acting made up for any vocal imperfections. God, that felt good, especially coming from this handsome, reserved guy. He's always been like that—my rock. We have our share of fights, but he is the most important thing in the world to me, the one thing I really rely on in this crazy life. Things have been going pretty well for me these days, but Jim's been having a terrible time. He hasn't been able to land an acting job in almost two years. He's bounced from one awful survival job to the next, sometimes unable to pay his half of the bills on time. He started smoking cigarettes again a couple of months ago. He's been pulling away from me, shutting me out. It's excruciating to see him so full of self-loathing. Today he had an audition for a musical. He was very much the type they needed and he'd worked really hard on the song they'd asked him to prepare. He thought he'd sung well, but they didn't even ask him to stay and read from the script. A wash-out.

It pushed him over the edge. He came home more depressed than I've ever seen him, telling me he was ready to call it quits and move back to Pittsburgh without me. He said he was sure I was only staying with him out of pity anyway. I told him that wasn't true, but he said he couldn't understand why I'd chosen him in the first place, why anyone would choose him. He feels profoundly unlovable. He's crying."

You've created an imaginary situation, drawn from meaningful experiences in your own life, based on your authentic feelings and needs, using the specifics of the lyric as your guidelines. You've carried your story through until it takes you right to the brink of the song.

There are two halves to this process: the preparation and the performance. Now you're ready to begin the

> When I do a musical theater piece, I'm looking for someone who can sing and act at the same time. You have to create believability, or you have nothing. You're asking an audience to suspend their disbelief long enough to accept the convention that people get up and sing in everyday life. In an audition, I want to hear what you can do vocally, yes, but I can do that with exercises. I want to hear you sing in character—yourself, a character, a character from the show you're auditioning for, depending on the situation. As a vocal coach, I work from the lyric and then go to the music, drawing connections between them; how a phrase of music should affect the way you approach the lyric, or vice versa, and how the musicality of the song really is in the words and in the character and in the scene. You'll find in the best theater songs, it is that absolute perfect marriage or melding of all those different elements—that the music and lyrics become inseparable.
>
> *Joseph Church,*
> *Musical Director/Composer*

performance, to speak the lyrics. Remember, your job in this song is to reassure your partner, to make him or her feel chosen and lovable.

D. Beginning The Performance

At this point you can either spend the time it takes to memorize the text, staying neutral and flexible, without locking into any particular way of saying the words, or you can gradually memorize the lines as you rehearse. Ultimately, of course, the song needs to be memorized, however you choose to do it.

There is an element of the process at this point that for most people requires professional guidance to master. That is the ability to speak simply and truthfully to another person, whether a flesh and blood actor or an imaginary partner, using the words of the playwright or lyricist, with no vocal acting, no phony line readings, no trying to put meaning into the words. Just plain, honest talking to someone using the words of the text. The best lesson I ever received in this concept happened years ago in Philadelphia. I was performing in a musical at night, and during the day there were rehearsals going on for the show coming in after us: a two-character play with the great Sandy Dennis as the star. (She memorably starred in a movie called "Up the

> I think that some singers hide behind the notes. They think that if they have great "money notes," if they're a spectacular singer, that they're going to get hired despite their weaknesses, and they don't move to correct the weaknesses by studying, going to an honest to God, down and dirty acting class. They'll go to Acting Class for Musical Theater. They'll go into a safe environment.
>
> Jim Wilhelm, Agent

Down Staircase," and won an Academy Award for playing Honey in the film version of "Who's Afraid of Virginia Wolf.") I used to sneak into the back of the theater and slouch down in a seat so I could watch her rehearse. The first day I did that I had a wild experience. Sandy Dennis, the other actor, and the director were up on the set discussing the scene. After several minutes the director clapped his hands a couple of times, walked off the stage into the house and said, "Ok, let's give it a go." At this point Sandy Dennis turned to the other actor and started talking. I had just seen her talking in real life, and since she was still speaking in the same natural way, I assumed she hadn't yet started the scene. But then the other actor responded to her and I heard a difference in his speech, a slight tinge of "performance." I knew immediately that he was acting, and then she responded to him in her absolutely natural way. I gasped, realizing that she was speaking the lines of the play, just as naturally as she'd spoken her own words in real life. I thought, "Well, there's what we're all after." Again Meisner's phrase: real living in imaginary circumstances. And without the ability to do that kind of simple, natural acting you'll be hard-pressed to bring a song to life organically. The ability to talk and listen in a scene in a truthful, unpushed way is the non-negotiable bottom-line ability required of an actor, whether in a TV commercial, Shakespeare or a Broadway musical. It's like needing to sit facing the keyboard in order to play the piano. I've seen acting classes where the teacher sits and for twenty minutes discusses with an actor what a scene is about, in complex Freudian terms. Then the actor stands up to work and every word that comes out of his mouth is phony and indicated, devoid of inner life or spontaneity. Forget it. Learn to work simply and authentically. Almost everyone needs an acting class to learn to do that. In my experience, the Meisner technique is the most effective way to learn the rudiments of acting. However you learn it, learn it.

E. The Opening Beat

Returning to "Why Did I Choose You?," we've engaged ourselves, turned ourselves on with our preparation, our daydream. We've involved ourselves in an imaginary situation in which a person we love deeply and have been with for many years is sitting in front of us in tears, feeling like the most unlovable loser on earth. Give yourself an Opening Beat, something that happens in your imaginary world immediately before you start to speak, which propels you into saying your first line. If it makes sense to have your imaginary partner ask you a question, have that happen, then you respond. You want your first line to be a reflexive response, a reaction to something. It could be someone walking away from you, a couple strolling by holding hands, the sun appearing from behind a cloud, someone spitting at you—whatever, just so that you don't have to try to pull your first moment out of thin air. In this case, what if your partner were to say, "Why the hell did you choose me in the first place?" Your reflexive response will be to say, "Why did I choose you?" And then you continue to speak the lyrics, always bearing this in mind: Your partner is the important one here, not you. Keep your focus on him or her and on accomplishing your goal. You want this person to calm down, to feel relief from their pain. Get your job done. Never mind yourself, how you look, how you sound, or even how you feel. Nobody cares how you feel, unless you're in pursuit of a goal. Your partner is the star as far as you're concerned. The irony here is that taking the focus off of yourself and putting it on someone else (whose emotional state is unacceptable to you) will make you a riveting presence. People will feel compelled to watch you, moved by you as you work against a powerful obstacle to get your job done. Conversely, the audience will not care about you if you're worried about your own appearance. You must care about your partner. Allow yourself to feel connected to and involved with your partner, whether it's a live person in a scene or an imaginary one at an audition. As a wise man once said: be the seer, not the seen. Don't worry about how you're coming off, how you're being seen. Be interested, not interesting. See something, something that engages you, moves you, challenges you and activates you, then act.

Choose a spot on a wall or somewhere across the room or theater and place your imaginary partner there, but do not fall into what I call Actor Eye-Lock. That is, don't glue your eyes onto the spot without ever looking away. Only actors and television news anchors do that. In life, when we're behaving spontaneously, we just about never do that. It's unnatural. I think it happens out of insecurity; trust that your partner will still be there if you look away, which you'll frequently need to do as you live moment to moment.

F. Tactics

Very often a performer will have a nice ability to believe in the imaginary world, will set up a terrific preparation that really turns them on emotionally, and will get beautifully launched into the monologue by an opening beat. Then, halfway through the piece they lose steam, lose their need to keep talking, and from there on the work is lifeless.

First of all, be sure that your imaginary situation is personal and important. High stakes are a must. Alfred Hitchcock once said "Movies are life with the boring parts cut out." That's true of songs as well. Be sure your obstacle is daunting, not easily surmountable. After all, if you could accomplish your objective easily, you wouldn't need a whole song—a line or two would do.

You have your partner. You have your objective. You have your obstacle and now you'll add something called Tactics: how you go about getting what you want. If I want someone to leave my apartment who insists on staying, I can try countless ways to get him out, even if I were to only use one line: "Get out of here." I can say it calmly and quietly. If that doesn't work I can say it with a laugh as if to say, "This is ridiculous—get out!" If that doesn't work I can whine like a baby. If that doesn't work I can drop to my knees and plead with him. If that doesn't work I can scream it. All are different ways to get my goal accomplished. Do your monologue with one objective, but with many different tactics. Not having enough tactics is most often what makes a performer run out of gas halfway through a song. Each and every line gives you an opportunity to try a new way to accomplish your goal. Each line has a meaning all its own. And this is important: expect that your tactics will work. Expect to win. When you realize you haven't yet won, you'll need to move forward into the next line, the next tactic, and your song will have a forward propulsion. In most cases you won't achieve your objective until the end of the song, if then. Need the whole song. But again, expect to win. To do otherwise is called "playing the problem." It's tedious watching someone who's not really trying to win, who's already resigned to losing.

There are different schools of thought regarding how to achieve a performance full of interesting, varied tactics. Some people believe it's best to map them out in advance, beat by beat, even writing them in the script: "tease…plead…seduce…demand…" Others believe that that's not a good idea, that if you've prepared well, believe fully in your imaginary circumstances, and have a strong objective and a formidable obstacle to overcome, you'll intuitively discover tactics as you proceed, just as we do in real life. Personally, I don't hold fast to either of these points of view. I think a combination of the approaches is most effective. There's a danger in the "scoring" technique of sending you up into your head, away from spontaneity. Even preplanned tactics need to feel as though they're happening impulsively. And sometimes working strictly improvisationally, with no decisions already made about tactics, can lead to shapeless, repetitive work. I suggest that you make some decisions beforehand regarding specific tactics on specific lines, but always work with an improvisational feel, being open to fresh and surprising uses of different words. Definitely be open to being fed and activated in unexpected ways by your fellow actors/characters, whether flesh and blood or imagined. Here's the goal: you want your work to be so emotionally true, and with so many surprising turns and tactics, that your audience will feel compelled to watch you. Work with real inner life and don't utter a word or a line that doesn't have a specific meaning. Don't allow your audience to look away from you for fear that they'll miss something.

I often begin working with actors who in real life conversation are, like most actors, very expressive, colorful, spontaneous and vivid in their communications. We'll discuss a song, speak the preparation out loud and then begin speaking the lyrics. But suddenly something odd happens. All of their natural color and expressiveness disappears. They speak the lyrics in a subdued, lifeless, extremely cautious way. They go from being engaged and interesting in real life to being bland and colorless once they enter the imaginary world and begin speaking. Let me reiterate, I definitely don't suggest that you start giving a big phony performance. Start easy, without pushing for meaning or emotion. It's very common for beginning actors to have the wind knocked out of them by a teacher who insists that they drop all of their phony "Look ma, I'm acting!" habits that served them so well in high school and community theater productions. And then these actors pick up a script and they're so scared of pushing and indicating that they leave their own natural expressiveness and theatricality out of it. Their work at this stage is honest but quiet, cautious and bland. It's then possible (and necessary) to allow the color, the passion, the expressivity back into the work. In fact, musical theater material demands

> You see a lot of actors taking a single acting beat and using it for a long stretch, sort of a generalized emotion. Being able to extend emotions over long periods is an important skill. But emotions are also complex, and in acting a capsule version of a scene in a song, you need to react to every word, listen to the person you're singing to, and be somewhat specific.
>
> *Joseph Church,*
> *Musical Director/Composer*

an enormous ability to be expressive. I once read an interview with Meryl Streep in which she was asked what other actresses had influenced her. She said that when she got to New York from Yale she went to see Liza Minelli in a Broadway musical called "The Act," and that it had been a revelation for her. Until then she hadn't realized that you could be that big and yet that truthful at the same time. You can. The characters, the human beings depicted in musicals are, by and large, overtly expressive people. They yell and scream and carry on and aren't good at hiding their feelings and needs. So it's necessary for actors in musicals to allow themselves to be their most expressive selves. After you've established within yourself a solid, consistent technique of simple, truthful, spontaneous acting, you need to live wildly and passionately within your imaginary situations. I think of musical theater as being closely aligned with classical theater. Plays by Shakespeare and songs in musicals have a lot in common—they both have metered, rhymed texts, and they both deal with expressive, passionate characters. It's essential to be able to connect emotionally within an imaginary situation, but you also need to be able to express your feelings and needs dynamically through the language of the play. In classical theater and in songs you must

> To me the best singer is the best actor. I mean you see that thing where someone's got their ear pressed to the door outside an audition room, panicking, saying, "I'm singing that song!" or "I'm doing that monologue!" But the truth of the matter is if they've done what they need to do there's no problem. Personalize, be inventive, make it like it's coming out of your mouth.
>
> Jordan Thaler, Casting Director

love the words and be able to use your voice and language to get what you want and express how you feel.

G. More About Preparation

I'd like to backtrack a minute and work through the preparation process on some other songs where it's a little trickier to decide upon a partner and an objective.

Look at "Being Alive" from "Company" by Stephen Sondheim:

Somebody hold me too close.
Somebody hurt me too deep.
Somebody sit in my chair,
And ruin my sleep,
And make me aware of being alive,
Being alive.

Somebody need me too much.
Somebody know me too well.
Somebody pull me up short,
And put me through hell,
And give me support for being alive,
Being alive,

Make me alive,
Make me confused,
Mock me with praise,
Let me be used,
Vary my days.
For alone is alone, not alive.

Somebody crowd me with love.
Somebody force me to care,
Somebody make me come through,

I'll always be there as frightened as you
To help us survive,
Being alive,
Being alive,
Being alive.

Listening to a run-through of the music lets us know that it's a surging, emotional ballad. Next we read the lyrics aloud in a simple way, just for the sense of them. We ask "What is this song about?" I'd say that "Being Alive" is about a person opening himself up to love and intimacy, welcoming it into his life, even though he's aware of all the pain it brings with it.

The script of "Company" is available, and if we were to study it we'd see that this character has, until this moment, been incapable of making a deep, authentic, intimate connection with anyone. Finally, after witnessing the permutations in his friends' relationships, and after his own ill-fated stabs at getting close to people, he's left better-informed but still lonely, unfulfilled and frustrated. He lists all his reasons for not getting close to someone. Then one of his friends, nudging him towards his breakthrough, says "…make a wish. Want something! Want something!" And this song is his response to that.

If asked to replace the song with a single line of dialogue I might come up with, "Please, somebody love me, even though it hurts like a son of a bitch." Then as a way of articulating my objective I could say, "If things go the way I want them to, after I sing this song someone will show up to love me." (Put these statements in economical, emotionally-charged ways. Remember that acting, like all art, is primarily an emotional experience rather than an intellectual one.) It's as if you say in this song, "Go ahead, do all the things I hate as long as I won't have to be alone anymore. I can't go on like this. Make me alive."

Then we'll set up "Being Alive," answering the questions: Who am I talking to? What do I want from them? What obstacle is in my way? The preparation here is not as simple as it was in "Why Did I Choose You?" You're not just talking to somebody else across the room. Yet you always want to be addressing somebody when you sing. It can be your mother, your lover, your nephew, your worst enemy. It can be a stadium full of people, it can be God, or it can even be one part of yourself addressing another part of yourself, i.e., the strong, loving adult in you comforting the frightened child in you. In the case of "Being Alive" you keep making appeals to "somebody." It's as if you're talking to your potential lover, as if somebody out there might hear your plea and answer you, come to you.

At the beginning of the song, you are alone, uninvolved with anyone, and you are desperately lonely. You haven't been willing to put up with all the intrusions and compromises and pains that having a relationship entails. In order to act this you need to access the part of yourself that pushes people away when they get too close, giving yourself "good reasons." Spin out a fantasy about it, basing it in your own experience. Make it a really bad scene: "I'm totally alone and I realize it's my own fault." Perhaps "It's Friday night, the end of a grueling week. I just saw someone I used to date whom I dumped. They were walking blissfully down the street arm in arm with a new lover. A long, lonely weekend lies ahead of me." Or maybe "It's New Year's Eve (or my birthday) and I've come home alone, with no one to share my life." Set up an imaginary situation in which your self-imposed aloneness comes up and hits you in the face. It's as if you find yourself at the bottom of a big black hole and you call out for help. "I speak these lyrics to an unseen, unknown person out there somewhere. I believe in this moment that someone may hear me and I hope and pray they'll respond to me." We're getting metaphysical with this preparation, but we're staying emotionally and psychologically true. What's the obstacle? They don't know you're here; they don't know you want them and need them. You have to let them know. Tell them you're here. Tell them what to do and what you need. In the song you make a list of all the off-putting things that people do to each other in relationships, and you say "Go ahead and do them!" Finally, you let them know what you have

> I remember working with a big male recording artist. He sang beautifully. But I remember going out to him and saying "I don't believe what you're saying. You seem very flip and slick and I don't think anybody's going to be moved by this. Nobody wants to hear you sing. They want to hear you tell a story through the song." We spoke about the lyric, about what we thought it meant. And his work changed immediately. He chewed it up. It's the best thing he ever recorded. I mean I don't think people buy records—I really mean this—I don't believe Sinatra was as big as he was, and remains to this day, I don't think they bought his records because he was a great singer. I think they bought his records because he was believable, singing the lyrics in the style he did. And I think that's the simplest answer. He was believable.
>
> Mike Berniker, Record Producer

to offer them: "I'll always be there as frightened as you to help us survive being alive." When they hear all that they're bound to show up. To kick you off (the opening beat) you might hear somebody say, "What is it you want?" so that your song is the answer to that question. Answering a question is a very effective way to get yourself into action. You always want to feel driven to speak.

Now get your job done. Remember to find each word, each sentence as you go along. Don't know what you're going to say next, what tactic you'll pull out next. In life we make it up as we go along. Let it be the same way in your monologue.

These songs are so great. They're expressions of elemental human life experiences. It's wonderful to connect to them as performers, to bring them to full emotional life, and it's wonderful for others to watch us do that.

Let's look at "A Quiet Thing" from "Flora the Red Menace" by Kander and Ebb:

When it all comes true,
Just the way you planned,
It's funny, but the bells don't ring.
It's a quiet thing.

When you hold the world
In your trembling hand,
You'd think you'd hear a choir sing.
It's a quiet thing.

There are no exploding fireworks,
Where's the roaring of the crowds?
Maybe it's the strange new atmosphere,
'Way up here among the clouds.

*But I don't hear the drums,
I don't hear the band,
The sounds I'm told such moments bring.
Happiness comes in on tiptoe.
Well, what d'ya know?
It's a quiet thing.
A very quiet thing.*

I think this lovely song is best handled as a talk with yourself. As I said earlier, one part of yourself can address another part of yourself. I could say that the action of the song is to convince myself that real love can be a quiet experience. In trying to arrive at an objective and an obstacle, look at it this way: the lyric keeps reiterating "It's a quiet thing." Why would I need to keep saying that? I'll set my world up so that it serves a real purpose to say those words. What if I've recently met someone and I seem to be falling in love, yet it's not a big flashy experience, and that concerns me? I've always expected that when I met the right person it would be like the 4th of July. A part of me believes I should be hearing a lot of wonderful explosions, but I'm not, so I'm worried. (This is a technique that can be very helpful: Give the opposing force, the obstacle, a voice. What would it have to say if it could speak?) Then I'd say the lyrics to that insecure part of myself to calm him down and restore his faith in this relationship. I'm singing to myself. My objective is my own confidence and peace of mind. My obstacle is my upset and doubt. Perhaps my opening beat could be hearing the insecure part of myself say, "But it's supposed to be all exciting!" Then I answer that voice with the song.

Let's look at "Someone to Watch Over Me" by the Gershwins:

There's a saying old says that love is blind,
Still we're often told "seek and ye shall find."
So I'm going to seek a certain lad I've had in mind.
Looking ev'rywhere, haven't found him yet;
He's the big affair I cannot forget –
Only man I ever think of with regret.
I'd like to add his initial to my monogram.
Tell me, where is the shepherd for this lost lamb?

[This opening section is called the verse. It's really an introduction to the main body of the song. Some songs have interesting, fleshed-out verses like this one. Some have discardable verses and some have none at all. The main body of the song is called the refrain or chorus:]

There's a somebody I'm longing to see.
I hope that he turns out to be
Someone who'll watch over me.

I'm a little lamb who's lost in the wood;
I know I could always be good
To one who'll watch over me.

Although he may not be the man some
Girls think of as handsome,
To my heart he'll carry the key.

Won't you tell him, please, to put on some speed,
Follow my lead? Oh, how I need
Someone to watch over me.

In deciding whom to sing this to and with what objective in mind, I would take my cue from the last section: "Won't you tell him, please, to put on some speed, follow my lead? Oh, how I need someone to watch over me." What if you thought of it as a prayer, a request of God, a Higher Power who has the ability to bring a loving companion into your life? I guarantee you, your performance of this song will be more compelling if you sing it to someone, pursuing an objective, rather than just using it as an expression of your loneliness. I could say, "In this song I'm asking God to bring me a lover who'll take care of me. If things go the way I want them to, after I sing this song God will agree to grant my request." When you're using an imaginary partner, know specifically who they are to you and *know what emotional condition they're in*. In "Why Did I Choose You?" your partner could be your cherished lover of fifteen years who is right now profoundly sad. In "Being Alive" your partner could be an unknown lover who's as frightened and lonely as you are. In "A Quiet Thing" your partner could be a part of yourself who is feeling frightened and anxious. In "Someone To Watch Over Me" your partner could be a powerful, loving Higher Power who is unaware of your needs and might even have some doubt about the validity of those needs. It's your partner and his/her feelings that are your concern as you perform. The energy of the performance comes from your attempt to resolve a conflict. Something is wrong in your imaginary world and you're using the song to make things right.

H. Celebration Songs

There's a certain kind of song that poses a particular challenge in terms of finding an objective and an obstacle: the song that's purely a celebration of good fortune. Examples are "Miracle of Miracles" from "Fiddler On the Roof," "I'm In Love With a Wonderful Guy" from "South Pacific," and "Oh

What a Beautiful Morning" from "Oklahoma." In these songs you're not making any obvious demands or requests. You're not instructing or comforting anyone. In fact, it seems that you're not even addressing anyone else. Yet all the principles that we've applied to the previous examples can be applied here also. Let's look at an example of this kind of song: "I Could Have Danced All Night" from "My Fair Lady", lyrics by Alan Jay Lerner, music by Frederick Loewe:

Bed! Bed! I couldn't go to bed!
My head's too light to try to set it down!

Sleep! Sleep! I couldn't sleep tonight!
Not for all the jewels in the crown!

I could have danced all night!
I could have danced all night!
And still have begged for more.

I could have spread my wings
And done a thousand things
I've never done before.

I'll never know what made it so exciting;
Why all at once my heart took flight.

I only know when he
Began to dance with me,
I could have danced, danced, danced all night!

Is it possible to find an objective and an obstacle in a song like this, which at first glance appears to contain neither element? Absolutely. Create a set up in which you're talking to someone who doesn't know, understand or appreciate what's happened to you and why you're feeling as you do. Your objective is his/her understanding and appreciation of you, and your obstacle is that he/she isn't "getting it." It's as if there's a little voice in you saying, "Don't you see? Don't you get it?" In fact, in "My Fair Lady" after Eliza sings the chorus for the second time, disregarding the reprimands of the maids who keep telling her to get to bed, the housekeeper Mrs. Pearce sings, "I understand, dear. It's all been grand, dear. But now it's time to sleep." Eliza gets what she's after. You simply get in touch with your need for other people's acknowledgment, understanding, and support—basic human needs.

I. Summary

And so the first step in the process of acting a song

> The cliché is that people in musicals can't act, but I think that is really old. I don't think that's the fact anymore. I think the musicals themselves are asking more, demanding more. Look at the people in Sondheim's pieces. Those are all great actors. You don't think of the performers in those shows as singers first. You think of them as actors first.
>
> *Scott Ellis, Director*

> There are people I can think of with gorgeous voices, who are very good-looking, but I still don't think they're going to get the parts they could if they learned to act. I think the lesson is Be who you are, even if you're not maybe who they thought they had in mind. Because there's a limit to how much you can change yourself, I think. The best thing to do in auditions, I think, is to say "Here I am, this is what I do. If I'm right, great. And if I'm not, fine. There'll be something else I am right for."
>
> *Ted Sperling, Conductor/Director/Orchestrator*

is to prepare and rehearse your song as a speech or monologue. To summarize the process so far:
- Write the lyrics out in paragraph form as if they were a speech.
- Listen to the music once or twice to get a sense of the emotional nature of the song.
- If the song is from a musical and the script is available, read it to find out what the dramatic context is for your song.
- Read the lyrics aloud simply, just to understand their sense.
- Begin your **preparation**. Ask, "What is this song about?" Answer with a single phrase that expresses a human action. "This song is about a person..." Write a line of dialogue that could replace the song, distilling its essence. (Most often the final lines of the song will reveal its core action.)
- Create an imaginary situation, based in your own experience, feelings and needs, that will require you to speak these words to someone. Tell yourself a story.
- Decide upon an **objective**. "If things go the way I want them to, after I sing this song..."
- Decide upon an **obstacle**. What would it say if it could speak? You have a job to get done—what's in your way? What **conflict** will this song resolve? What serious consequences will you suffer if you don't achieve your objective?
- Set up your circumstances so that the opposite of what you want exists at the beginning of the song. Look out into your imaginary world—something is not as you

wish it to be. You'll use the song to correct things, to make them right.

- Create an **opening beat** for yourself, an event that triggers you, propels you into speaking the first line. You want the opening line to be a response to something.
- You can either take the time to memorize the text at this point or you can gradually memorize it as you rehearse.
- Now that you're emotionally turned on in your imaginary world, with a job you need urgently to accomplish and an obstacle in your way, speak the lyrics to your imaginary partner (whether that's your spouse, your mother, a stadium full of people, God, or a part of yourself). Speak the lyrics to make something happen—remember, your partner is the important one as far as you're concerned.
- Rehearse the monologue, always with an improvisational feel, and with a tremendous variety of tactics, using each line in a fresh way to achieve your objective—one objective, many tactics.

As I said earlier, my experience has been that a good acting teacher is required in order to learn to work organically and deeply on a consistent basis. I encourage you to bring any additional acting techniques you've learned to bear on this part of the work. If you're in an acting class that includes monologue work, why not work on the song lyric, sans music, in the class? Take advantage of every opportunity to bring the lyrics to life.

The Rhythm

The next step is adding the rhythm. You'll need to have a pianist record the accompaniment of the song for you, and get whatever help you need to learn the rhythms to which the composer has set the lyrics. Learn them well and learn them precisely. In the musical theater it's customary to honor the composer's decisions to the letter regarding rhythm and melody. Even if you're working in venues where there's more leeway to "make the song your own" by modifying the music, such as cabaret or jazz, it's still a good idea to learn what the composer intended before you start changing things. Even Ella Fitzgerald, on her classic "Song Book" albums, generally sings a song once through just as it's written, and then she'll sing it again with her own variations.

> Well, when I teach music I have a basic plan that I generally like to follow: I like to teach it slowly and incredibly accurately from the start. I find that if somebody glosses over something early on that they're likely never to get it right.
> *Ted Sperling, Conductor/Director/Orchestrator*

> When I watch performers I look for a natural kind of phrasing; it should be acted. When it's just sung, there's nothing there.
> *Lynn Ahrens, Lyricist/Librettist*

Play the tape of the accompaniment and begin speaking the lyrics in rhythm. The melody is not yet of any concern—just extend your natural speech to fit the rhythms as written.

In general, stepping into the rhythm will slow you way down from the tempo in which you speak in everyday conversation. Do not just speak the words at your normal pace and then wait for the music to "catch up" before you speak the next line. Speak…in…the…pace…of…the…song's…tempo. Feel the music's pulse. Any words that are set on notes of extended duration, words which when eventually sung will be "held out," must be held out now, as in "I could have da-a-a-anced all ni-i-i-ight…" As you begin moving through the lyrics like this, doing the rhythmic line reading, talking-in-the-rhythms-the-composer-has-set, exte-e-e-ending the words that get extended, you will probably feel ridiculous and you'll hope your neighbors can't hear you. But here's the point: When the circumstances of our real lives become extraordinary we use our voices in extraordinary ways. When the flame under our emotions gets turned up high, we use language in unusual ways. As I've said, songs aren't about ordinary, insignificant moments in our lives; they're about intensely important moments. If you listen to people who are in extreme emotional situations, you'll hear them speak in ways they normally don't. Let the imaginary circumstances you've set up for your song be so important that they force you to speak the lyrics in the super-expressive rhythms laid out by the composer. Make a breakthrough into letting your experience be huge; let your expression of the lyrics be an exceedingly big experience. Be that emotional, that big, that expressive. Embarrass yourself. Often singers shy away from being engaged in the experience of the song to the full extent required to justify their speaking the words in the preordained rhythms at the preordained tempo. Go for it. Let yourself be ridiculously expressive. And prepare yourself. When you really let yourself be so involved in your imaginary world that you live in those rhythms, you will inevitably have a deep emotional experience. Most big stars are willing to do that and that's why people flock to watch them work. We all love to watch other people at full emotional throttle—it stirs our own deep emotions.

Another element comes into play in this rhythmic part of the process. In most songs there will be durations of time when the accompaniment plays but the voice "lays out." In some songs there's a lot of extended space with no singing. In "I Believe In You" from "How to Succeed In Business Without Really Trying" by Frank Loesser, after the lyrics: "You have the cool, clear, eyes of a seeker of wisdom and truth," there are two and a half measures of rests. In the verse to "I'm in Love With a Wonderful Guy" from "South Pacific" by Rodgers and Hammerstein, there are seven bars of singing: "I expect ev'ryone of my crowd to make fun of my proud protestations of faith in romance" and then seven bars of rests. These are extreme cases, but almost all songs have some spots where the accompaniment plays and you don't sing. Whenever this situation arises, it's your job to fill that time with life. The last thing you want to do is to stand there like Bambi in the headlights waiting for your next line. Find creative ways to use the rests—need the rests. Set it up so that they're assets, not liabilities. There are many ways of doing this. You can use the time between sung phrases to search inside yourself for your next tactic; you can use it to put a nonverbal closure on what you've just said; you can imagine that your partner speaks, or looks away, or throws you a dirty look, to which you respond with your next line. However you do it, fill it, always being open to reversals, emotional shifts, changes in direction, surprises. In this way you'll make yourself as compelling to the audience when you're not singing as when you are.

One additional point: what applies to the music between your lines definitely applies to any music that occurs before you sing—the introduction. Whether it's a bell tone, a simple arpeggio, a four-bar introduction, or pages of orchestral music, as often happens in opera, your life must start with the first note of accompaniment. Don't stand uninvolved during the introduction and then suddenly come to life when you sing. Use the introduction. Fill it. Need it. Any and all music is a reflection of your imaginary world, and it's your job to justify it. While the introduction plays, be alive in your situation. Let it reflect your opening beat. Perhaps your imaginary partner speaks to you during it. Let yourself react nonverbally. It's great to have reversals occur even before you start singing. An audience will immediately think, "Oh, this one I have to watch. They're going to be full of surprises and I don't want to miss anything." Be alive and reactive during the introduction, even before you start singing.

So your monologue is on its feet in this new, expanded way. All the guidelines we discussed earlier are still relevant: work impulsively, improvisationally—live it. Think of yourself as choosing this way of saying the words. When you extend a vowel, let it be infused with the meaning of the word all the way through. Love the words and get everything you can out of them as you strive to accomplish your objective. If they came to you and said, "We want you to drop all those rhythms and just speak it normally" you'd say, "No way! I need to speak it that way to make my points. It's too important for me to drop the rhythms!" And be sure to let your tactics be infinitely varied. The path of your monologue mustn't be a straight line. It needs to go in many different, surprising directions, just like happens in life. Don't grab onto one big old feeling and try to ride it through to the end of the song. Find each new thought as you go—let yourself be as surprised as anyone at what you come up with next. Think about what you're saying as you say it. Let every sound you make be infused with inner meaning. As always, want something from someone very badly, have an obstacle in your way, and use each line, each word, each syllable to obtain your goal, using the composer's specific rhythms to help you express yourself.

The Melody

Now we're ready for the final step: adding the melody. Remember I said earlier that all human speech is melodious. The range of pitches we employ in our everyday conversation is relatively narrow, not much beyond a five or six-note span in the lower-middle part of our vocal range. Yet we are capable of making vocal sounds over a much wider range of pitch. If you listen to someone in a highly-charged, emotional conversation, you'll probably hear pitches much higher and lower than normal. Our emotions naturally propel our voices into extremes of highs and lows. If you heard someone emoting in a real-life conversation up on a high A, then you asked her to sing a phrase with an A in it, she probably wouldn't be able to do it unless she was an experienced singer. Her mind, her limited sense of her own potential would stop her, even though her emotion had carried her up to high notes effortlessly. It makes sense that songs will have melodies outside a normal speaking range since songs, as we've said, are about extraordinary situations.

It certainly behooves any singer to study voice with a good teacher who can help them produce a strong, flexible sound in a healthy, reliable way. But when you're actually out there performing, you need to be able to take your vocal technique for granted. A great athlete works out and goes through drills for countless hours in preparation for a game. But once he's out there playing he's alive in the moment, not thinking about his technique. It may be necessary to have a certain amount of concentration on your vocal production as you perform a song, but those thoughts need to be way on the back burner if you're to effectively act the song, to live it with real emotion.

So we add the specific pitches of the song, the melody, to the monologue-in-rhythm. As you see, the steps I outline are cumulative—we keep adding elements to what we've already accomplished. Here we are at the final stage: We're singing the song. The object in this melody step is to justify speaking the lyrics at these pitches, many of them being outside your normal speaking range.

> People buy records because they're moved by what is being said to them, not by what's being sung to them.
> *Mike Berniker, Record Producer*
>
> In terms of musical theater, we full well know there are a lot of great voices out there, but if all they have are great "money notes," it's not enough. We'll generally pass on those people. We want people who can act.
> *Jim Wilhelm, Agent*

How many times a week do you speak in real life up on an E or a G or a high B flat or down on a low G? Not very often, unless you live a strange and dramatic life. But once in a while, when you're in extreme circumstances, you speak on extreme pitches. Give yourself a D or an E up at the top of your middle range if you're a man, or a B flat above middle C if you're a woman, and say a few words up there. Do you see how emotionally charged you'd have to be to need to speak that high? Well, that's how charged your imaginary circumstances need to be. Let them be so important and let yourself get so engaged in them that those pitches come out of you organically. Have a big experience when you sing. I had a voice teacher who called singing "cultivated yelling." Pavarotti has called it "screaming on pitch." Most characters who sing aren't afraid to yell. In "Carousel," Billy Bigelow at the end of his "Soliloquy": "I'll go out and make it or steal it, or ta-a-a-ake it, or di-i-i-ie!" He's yelling. In "South Pacific," Nelly Forbush singing "I'm in love, I'm in love, I'm in love, I'm in love, I'm in love with a wonderful guy!" She's yelling. Of course, it's not all yelling. "I've Grown Accustomed to Her Face" in "My Fair Lady" doesn't involve any yelling. It contains a different kind of fervent intensity. But I guarantee, most songs will require you to let 'er rip. An operatic soprano once came to me with the intention of learning to bring some acting values to her singing. She understood that she'd be more effective if she were emotionally involved with her arias. We worked for several sessions and the same thing kept happening: I'd talk to her, explaining my approach and laying out the steps. She'd listen intently, nodding to express her comprehension and willingness to do as I suggested. Then she'd stand up to begin working through an aria and she'd be lifeless and bland. After spending a couple of sessions with her something dawned on me and I said to her, "In life you're very quiet and subdued, aren't you?" She said, "Yes, I've always been very shy and reserved." I pointed out to her that while she was like that, the operatic characters she was portraying, trying to bring to life, were screaming drama queens. If she were going to really live in this material she'd have to be willing to behave in a way that she was not willing to behave in her daily life. You need to allow yourself to be your very most expressive self when you work on your songs. Characters who sing are people who "live out loud." They're radically expressive and so that's what you must be to act them.

There's more about adding the melody, but let me interject this first: Most of us need to take the advice I gave to that opera singer. You may be someone who's had a rough history with romantic relationships and so, to avoid pain, you don't let yourself get involved anymore. Well, you must be willing to "get involved" romantically when it comes to your acting and singing or you won't be able to sing love songs with any reality or depth. (And I'm afraid most songs are love songs.) If you're someone who would never express anger forthrightly, or plead to have your needs met, or toss off a sarcastic crack, you need to be willing to do those things within the imaginary world in which you perform. You must be willing to sometimes be in your performing what you don't allow yourself to be in real life, or you'll seriously limit your range of expression. You have a huge range of life and expression inside. Give yourself an imaginary situation that will call it forth. Play the game.

Back to the melody. As you sing the song, placing the words on the prescribed pitches, use the pitches to make your points. Choose the melody, just as you choose the words and the rhythms. It needs to feel as though you're creating the song as you go along. As far as you're concerned, there aren't "high notes." There are just important things you need to communicate, and sometimes the only way to make your point is to pitch a word way up high or way down low. In "Why Did I Choose You?" the word "you" in the first sentence is the highest pitch. Make sense of that as you sing it. Need the word to be said that high. By the time you get to the last part of the song you're way up on an F when you say, "I lost it lovingly and willingly to you." You're practically yelling it. Love the words, love the rhythms, and love the melody. They serve you as you express your inner life, as you communicate, as you strive to make things the way you want them in your imaginary world.

> A song is simply an extension of the speech of the scene.
>
> Lynn Ahrens, Lyricist/Librettist

Let me say here a word about your diction when you sing. Often at this point of the process I'll hear a singer pronouncing the words with extra "good" diction. Lots of consonants show up that they'd never articulate in everyday speech. In fact, it's not good diction, it's just the exaggerated speech that most of us learn to use when singing in choirs. In choirs it is necessary to over-pronounce, but for somebody singing a solo song, it's an impediment to the acting. Unless you're working on a song that requires some kind of upper-crust dialect, do not elevate your diction when you sing. Sing the words like you talk them, allowing that your normal speech isn't inarticulately sloppy. This can be a hard habit to break. I had a tough time with it myself. Break it. Sing like yourself. They'll understand you, and you'll have an easier time being real.

Music itself has emotional resonance and it will affect your work as you add it to the mix. You can count on being activated emotionally by just the music. Allow it to move you, to get inside of you. In fact, here's an exercise that can help you a lot: Sing the song strictly as a sensory experience. Drop the words—you might want to close your eyes and sing it on "la, la, la…" or hum it. Let your body move to it. Dance around a bit. Don't think at all of the lyrics; just make the music as if you were the lead instrument in a band or orchestra. Enjoy it. Create it as you go along. See what the song feels like just as a piece of music. I was working with a talented young actor once. I gave him a beautiful ballad from "Plain and Fancy" called "Young and Foolish" to work on. I had a sense he could soar with it. He worked through all the steps and his work was okay, but he wasn't making an exciting emotional connection. I had him do the exercise of making the music without any concentration on the lyrics, and he got set on fire by the beauty and feeling of the music alone. He sang it like Yehudi Menuhin playing the violin. Then he sang it again with the words, but this time he made a huge emotional connection, the tears streaming down his face. Give it a try with your own songs.

Gestures and Focus

In discussing gestures, body language, and focus, I would say this in general: preplanning your gestures is usually counter-productive. It tends to send you right into your head and inhibits spontaneity. In real life you don't worry about your "gestures" when you're talking to someone. Don't worry about them when you're singing a song. Ideally, your performance of a song is a natural, living, breathing, dynamic experience: "real living in imaginary circumstances." If you find yourself feeling awkward and self-conscious physically when you sing, if you "don't know what to do" with your hands, my suggestion is that you put more time, energy, and heart into your preparation. If you're concentrating on your objective, if you allow yourself to really care about the state your imaginary partner is in, if you work one beat at a time, finding tremendous variety in your tactics, you will instinctively use your body to help you make your points. Sometimes you'll find yourself staying very still as you sing, sometimes you'll move your body, lift an arm, take a walk, point a finger—movements that emphasize ideas, just as you do when you're talking in real life. Again, if you feel self-conscious physically, it's an indication that you are not engaged in, immersed in your imaginary world. Engage yourself. Immerse yourself by preparing, daydreaming about people, places, and things you really care about. Tell yourself a story that demands you take action to remedy something. Then use the song, your language, your voice and your body to accomplish your objective.

I would add that it is possible to be given "blocking," specific movements, even choreography, and to fulfill those physical requirements organically. The brilliant director/choreographer Bob Fosse blocked numbers down to the fingertips, but the great performers he worked with, beginning with Gwen Verdon, brought the blocking to life, infused it with their own personalities and feelings and needs. It was as if they themselves were making it up as they went along. (Fosse and Verdon both studied acting with Sanford Meisner and brought a tremendous sense of truth to their work.) Sometimes in your rehearsals you'll find yourself gesturing or moving in ways that help you express certain ideas, and you may choose to repeat those movements in later performances of the song. That's great, so long as they don't become empty, intellectual, indicated movements. Stay open to new experiences; always, in that sense, be improvising.

As far as where to look, where to focus your gaze, there are some practical considerations. Obviously, for the most part you'll work facing your audience. It's fine to turn upstage for a moment if that's part of what you need to do as you work through your tactics, but, after all, we are doing this for the audience's benefit. So when you're alone on stage or at an audition, face front. If you're singing to an actual person on stage with you, find ways to be in contact with your partner while still honoring the need of the audience to see you. When you're alone, I believe it's best to picture your imaginary partner just above the heads of the listeners if you're in a studio, or at the level of the first balcony if you're in a theater. The point is to have a slightly elevated face so that the audience gets a good look at you. I strongly discourage you from looking spectators in the face. There are exceptions to every rule and, occasionally, you'll sing a song that really works best if sung right to the people in the room. Once in a while a director will even ask you to sing right to him or her. Obviously, honor that request. But in general it's a bad idea for several reasons. For one thing, they're not rehearsed actors who'll be able to enter the scene with you and give you what you need emotionally, so they're likely to throw you right out of your imaginary world. In addition, if they think you're looking right at them, they'll feel obligated to somehow be a part of your acting experience and they shouldn't be asked to do that—it makes them feel very uncomfortable. They need to be able to just watch you, observe you, and appraise your work. A singer I work with recently told me that she was waiting with a group of other actors to be called in to sing her song, and out of the audition room stormed the casting director, who bellowed, "People! People!! I am not you acting partner! Do not look at me when you sing!!" Yikes.

Generally, it's also not a good idea to set up an empty chair and then sing

> I hate being looked at in auditions. Some actors tend to make eye contact, and it makes me very uncomfortable, or they sing right to you, and they always pick me for some reason. Probably just because I'm trying to smile at them. Most actors learn to focus beyond you, and I prefer that. It's easier to look at them, because otherwise you have to respond—they're asking something of you, and it's not anything you can give in that moment.
>
> Lynn Ahrens, Lyricist/Librettist

to that. Again, I recommend you place an imaginary partner just above the heads of your audience. That way they'll have just one point of focus in their sight line—you.

Character Acting

There are certain roles in the musical theater that are called "character parts." These are portrayals of people who are in various ways quirky, colorful or out of the ordinary—characters other than the straight ahead, good-looking leading men and women such as Curly in "Oklahoma" and Marian the Librarian in "The Music Man." If you happen to be naturally quirky, colorful, and out of the ordinary, you'll probably be able to fall right into roles like Hysterium in "A Funny Thing Happened On the Way to the Forum," Adelaide or Nathan in "Guys and Dolls," Anita in "West Side Story," Miss Hannigan in "Annie" or the M.C. in "Cabaret." The list of juicy character roles goes on and on and, as I said, if you were born somehow offbeat, the songs written for these characters may come easily and naturally to you. It could be your niche. The central question here is: Can you perform the song by basically just behaving as yourself within the imaginary circumstances or does the material require you to behave differently than you do walking around in your life? By that I mean is the character exaggerated in some way: mean and cranky, wildly theatrical, ridiculously naive, sneaky and manipulative, hysterically nervous? Does the character need to have a funny, squeaky voice, or speak in a dialect? When the song you're singing requires you to be significantly different from how you are normally, you will need to make a **character adjustment**. A character adjustment can be physical, as in an accent or any unusual way of producing your voice, like making it nasal or raspy. It can be a way of using your body as in a limp or a swagger, or it can be primarily psychological or emotional, as in being paranoid or vindictive or silly and care-free. The trick for the actor is to make the adjustment, the adaptation away from who you normally are, and then to just let it be, to inhabit the character while you act the song the way you would any song, with a partner, an objective, an obstacle, tactics—the whole works.

There are some brilliant examples of character acting by movie actors. For their roles in "Kramer vs. Kramer," neither Dustin Hoffman nor Meryl Streep needed to make character adjustments. They both lived as themselves within the given circumstances of that movie. But they've both given incredible performances where they had to transform themselves. Think of Hoffman as Ratso Rizzo in "Midnight Cowboy" or as that "woman" in "Tootsie." He has an amazing ability to make wild character adjustments and then to live fully and organically in the scenes. There are numerous dazzling character performances in the movie "The Wizard of Oz." Think of Bert Lahr as the Cowardly Lion or Margaret Hamilton as the Wicked Witch. Wow!

I've seen actors who could not catch fire in a particular song until they made a character adjustment, and then they sprang to life. They were rather dull when they played it as "themselves," but they were immediately engaging when they somehow adapted themselves. An adjustment can free some actors to actually use and reveal more of themselves. It's important that actors get to know and accept themselves as they really are. If you're a sort of dancing banana, use that in your songs when you can. Charles Nelson Reilly became a star by simply being his funny, goofy self. If you're not that unusual but do have a knack for making character adjustments and then really living in imaginary circumstances, find material where you can show that ability off. Certain material will simply not work unless played by idiosyncratic "characters": some of Noel Coward's songs, most of the roles in "A Funny Thing happened On the Way to the Forum," Judd in "Oklahoma," the Old Lady in "Candide," Fosca in "Passion." If this kind of character work is not your bag, so be it. The truth is that most stars are not character actors—they do not adapt themselves much in their roles. They latch on to something deep and central in their own personalities and bring that to light in performance after performance.

> I got a call from Disney. They wanted me to come out to L.A. because Tony Jay, who was playing the villain in [the animated movie] "Hunchback," a brilliant British actor, was unable to sing his high notes. He wanted to take everything down an octave. So I walk in and he's singing in this tortured, pushed way. He's got a great voice, but he's not an experienced singer. He said, "This is too high. I can't do this." And I said, "Singing is speech. When you speak you are going up and down, depending on what you're saying, depending on the emphasis. There's a melody to speech. Now what this song is asking you to do is say these words *up here*. What would be in front of you that would cause you to speak there?" And because he was a great actor, he just put something in front of him, and out came the phrase. Every time he'd miss a note I'd say, "Change what's in front of you."
>
> *David Friedman,*
> *Composer/Lyricist/Conductor*

AUDITIONS

I'LL DEAL NOW WITH AUDITIONING for the musical theater. First and foremost, I can tell you from having been involved as either the musical director or accompanist at hundreds of auditions, that by and large the performers who make the biggest impact, the ones who rivet the attention of the listeners and get callbacks and jobs are the ones who can act. They are the ones who come into the room, deal professionally with the auditors and with the accompanist, and then immerse themselves in an imaginary world in which they make real emotional contact with an imaginary partner and use the song to accomplish an objective. All the external finesse and polish in the world isn't worth a nickel if you're not truly living, here and now, within the world of your song. God knows there have been performers who've had musical theater careers without being able to act organically. Sometimes the precision and audacity of their indicating gets them hired; sometimes having an extraordinarily beautiful or powerful voice gets them hired. But those people are the exceptions, and I guarantee you they'd go even further if they found a way to make true emotional connections to their material.

Auditioning is a craft unto itself. There are performers who do a great job once they're in rehearsals and performances but who get hung up when it comes to auditioning. The tension of having to make a fast, strong, positive impression in the pressurized situation of an audition can help some people to score but can be daunting to others.

An audition is essentially a job interview. It's helpful to put your energy into the things you have control over and not into the things that are out of your control. You can't do anything about who will be judging you, their attitude or response to you, the size and shape of the room, the proficiency of the pianist. You can take charge of your preparation for the audition, your own attitude and your behavior in the room. The auditors will be looking at you from two directions: how good is your work and are you someone they'd want to work with? Their judgement of you starts the moment you enter: Is he/she confident, well-prepared and put together, easy to get along with, flexible, open to suggestions and directions, an adult, gracious and courteous? Even though you may feel like you're walking into a battle, the auditors want you to do well. They're looking for allies, performers who will help bring their project to life. You want them to want to work with you. Be warm and courteous but not overly friendly or chatty. In general don't ask questions of the auditors, such as "What would you like me to sing?" You make that decision before you enter the room. Sometimes there are exceptions; if you know a song from the show you're auditioning for you can say "I have a song from the show. Would you like to hear that or would you prefer something else?" But in general keep any demands of the auditors to an absolute minimum; they have many people to deal with and the last thing they're looking for are needy, high-maintenance performers. Also, don't apologize for anything before you begin. If you have a cold or had a late night, keep it to yourself.

Be as well-prepared as you possibly can, so that those

few minutes in the audition room will be everything they can be. I don't think it's a good idea to learn new songs for each audition. Have a carefully chosen repetoire of songs that show you off in different ways and that you know very well. I can tell you from experience that most performers who repeatedly get hired for principle roles in the New York musical theater have just a few songs—often only three or four—that they use at every audition. They find a couple of pieces of material that are perfectly suited to them, that allow them to reveal in two or three minutes some essential parts of themselves, emotionally and vocally. The song may be a big splashy vocal showpiece that displays sass and irreverence; it may be a warm, courageous anthem, or even a self-deprecating lament. I've seen leading Broadway players go into audition after audition leading off with "their" song, even if it's not stylistically right on the money for the particular show they're going in for. Be on the lookout for that kind of material for yourself—songs that when

> The people I remember from auditions are the ones who came in with confidence, without being cocky; they had prepared a very straight-forward song that showed them off to advantage. And you know what? They showed joy in the audition. I would say that's a big thing for me, for almost anything. I like to see someone for whom I feel singing is an exhilarating experience, and who can communicate that kind of relaxed quality at an audition: "This is me, this is how I sound. If I'm right, great. If I'm not, fine." If someone is comfortable with him or herself, and is relaxed, you can tell, and that is the most appealing thing to me.
>
> *Ted Sperling, Conductor/ Director/Orchestrator*

you hear them or sing them make you say, "That's me! That was written for me!" Be able to answer this question without missing a beat: If you had an audition today and had to sing your best up-tempo and ballad, the ones that best show you off, what two songs would they be? At the same time I do recommend that you develop a full repertoire of audition material so that you can give the auditors things that they need to hear stylistically. Ideally every song you choose to make a part of your audition repertoire will be a home run, a song that you love and that shows you off in a big way.

I also think it's a good idea to have a mix of well-known standards and less familiar songs in your kit. There really are no hard and fast rules about this. I know people who get jobs singing totally obscure, sometimes eccentric material, and I know a woman who's gotten into numerous Broadway shows singing "Summertime," which most people will tell you to never use because of its over-familiarity. Often at auditions a performer will make a good impression with his or her first piece, which may well be a song not frequently heard. Then the director will ask to hear a war-horse such as "Oh, What a Beautiful Morning" or "I Got Rhythm" because there are certain things they can tell immediately from material they know inside and out. As I said, put together a repertoire that includes both familiar and unfamiliar songs. As always, the bottom line is how well you're able to work expressively with an inner life.

I learned an important lesson some years ago when I was the accompanist for a whole week's worth of auditions for several major summer stock theaters. During that week one song that I heard over and over was "Fifty Percent," a powerful ballad originally sung by Dorothy Loudon in "Ballroom." By the third day I had decided that none of my people should use that song for a while because it was losing its impact by being heard so often. Then at the end of the week another woman came in and led off with "Fifty Percent," but her performance of it was a revelation—vocally a knockout, but more importantly full of emotion and humor and urgency, performed absolutely as if she were making it up as she went along. It was as if we had never heard the song before and she got a well-deserved callback. Certainly I would be wary of leading off with a song that's done to death, but if you bring something personal, unique and powerful to it, by all means use it.

In New York there are voice teachers and vocal coaches. The difference between them is that the teacher's job is to help you produce the sound in a healthy, effective way while a coach's job is to help you find songs, teach you the music if you're not a trained musician, set up your music professionally so that other pianists can play it, and hopefully assist you in the acting of the songs. With the help of a knowledgeable vocal coach build yourself a collection of wonderful audition songs. I have found that the most efficient way to proceed with this is to lay out a chart on a legal pad that includes all the various categories of songs for which you might be asked. It might look like this: (I'll list some examples of standard songs for each category. Note that some songs can do duty in more than one category.)

Broadway Up-Tempo

Miracle of Miracles (man)
Luck Be a Lady (man)
I Could Have Danced
    All Night (woman-legit)*
Johnny One-Note (woman-belt)

Contemporary/Pop Up-Tempo**

My Life (by Billy Joel)
A Little Help From
    My Friends (by the Beatles)

30s/40s Standard Up-Tempo

Lady Is a Tramp
They All Laughed

Character/Comedy

Miracle of Miracles
Adelaide's Lament
I Cain't Say No

50s Rock and Roll

Rockin' Robin
Rock Around the Clock

Broadway Ballad

Younger Than Springtime (man)
If Ever I Would Leave You (man)
Till There Was You (woman-legit)
What I Did For Love (woman-belt)

Contemporary/Pop Ballad

Bridge Over Troubled Water
All In Love Is Fair
    (by Stevie Wonder)

30s/40s Standard Ballad

Night and Day
My Funny Valentine

Sondheim***

The Miller's Son
Finishing the Hat
Nothing's Gonna Harm You

Country

Crazy
Tennessee Waltz

---

   * Some Women have the ability to sing in soprano range (referred to as "legit") and to sing in chest voice ("belt") and they'll want to delineate "Broadway Up-Tempo/Ballad Legit" and "Broadway Up-Tempo/Ballad Belt."
 ** I suggest looking in the world of commercial pop and rock for these songs. You'll find a lot of very theatrical songs there. The Broadway repertoire for this category is not vast and tends to be over-used.
*** This guy's work is so exceptional that he rates his own slot.

In the interest of seeing as many singers as possible, sometimes the people running an audition won't allow you to sing your full songs, and so you'll need to be ready with portions of songs (usually "16 bars," sometimes, alas, only "8 bars"). For a chorus call, the general rule is "high and loud."

> When I'm casting something, the biggest turn-on for me is when a performer comes and first, goes to work—is not concerned about the result of the audition, and I can feel that right away. It's a turn-off to me. "How'm I doing? Do you like me?" Hate that.
>
> Rob Marshall,
> Director/Choreographer

It's possible and important to incorporate all of your acting technique even when you're only singing a short section of a song. Prepare and rehearse your shorter segments as though they were complete entities unto themselves.

Regarding the keys in which you sing: again, no hard and fast rules. If you're auditioning for a production of "My Fair Lady" in a summer stock theater, they'll probably need to hear you sing from the score in the original keys. But in general, sing your audition material in the keys that are best for you personally, the keys that serve both your singing and acting requirements. Fiddle around with a pianist or coach until you figure out what keys are best for you. Don't be afraid to change the keys from where they're published. In most cases, those published keys were either the keys found to have worked best for the original performers, or they're the ones found to be the easiest for the publishers to work with on the printed page. Warning: You'll sabotage yourself if you ask an accompanist at an audition to transpose at sight. Have the music written out fully in your key. (You can find people who do this at rea-

> I tell people to find songs that reveal who they are. Also, first of all, it saves you time—you don't have to then learn a new piece for every audition, which I see a lot of people feeling the need to do, and it's daunting. They're in a panic, and they go in, they don't know it as well, they haven't experienced auditioning with it enough, because I think that counts for a lot. I think you have to go to a million auditions, and you should do basically a small repertoire at all of them until you refine it and feel expert at it; songs that sound like you, that express your outlook a little bit.
>
> *Ted Sperling, Conductor/Director/Orchestrator*

sonable cost on computer programs.) Sometimes you can get away with having the proper chord symbols written in red above the untransposed music, but even that is risky. Have your music professionally prepared: in the right key, cut to the proper length, copied on hard paper (card stock) and taped together, or in a binder—be careful of plastic covers, which can reflect light and make it hard for the pianist to see the music. Never plop down a big book of published music on the piano; it's likely to not stay open and fall into the accompanist's lap. Have the music copied and keep copies of your audition songs somewhere safe at home, in case you lose the originals.

One other crucial consideration when choosing songs for your audition book is the difficulty factor of the piano parts. Unless you're bringing your own pianist to the audition you must make sure that the songs you're using aren't too hard for the pianist to sight-read. It can really break your heart to find a song that's great for you, only to then realize that you can't include it in your book due to the difficulty of the piano part,

Auditions

but you're asking for a train wreck if you don't take that into consideration. The best thing to do is to ask your coach or another pianist for their advice.

Spend the time and money to have professional, up-to-date pictures and resumés. Have an idea of roles you think you're right for. Keep a written list of them in your audition binder. Know what basic type you are (leading man/lady, juvenile/ingénue, character actor, or some combination of these). Think of established performers to whom you're similar. It's good to know these things for yourself and to have them at the ready should you be asked to describe yourself.

You may be asked to come back for a dance audition or to read from a script. You can develop the ability to pick up choreography quickly and to do well with a cold reading by attending classes or working with coaches.

Dress appropriately. Usually it's best to wear something stylish and attractive, as if you were going to a special party. If the show has a particular style or feel, you can suggest that in your clothing. Don't wear a costume, but you can try to show something of the essence of the show. If it's "Les Miserables" or "Fiddler on the Roof" you can dress a little bit "peasanty," if it's rock and roll, a little funky, etc. Look great, whatever you choose to wear. Remember, an audition is a form of a job interview.

Practice your songs in front of other people before

> I hope to see someone who has an idea about what the songs are about, other than just singing the notes and making a decent sound—someone who'll have an interpretive idea about the song that's interesting and truthful and personal. That's for starters.
>
> *Stephen Holden, Critic*

you take them into auditions. Take a class where you can sing in front of a group on a regular basis, or organize a group yourself, hire a pianist and get together each week to sing for each other. Singing alone or in front of your teacher or coach is one thing, but once you're in that room auditioning with other people watching you'll experience a whole new set of nerves. Put yourself in situations where you're being watched by other people before you get to the audition so that those nerves can come up and be dealt with. My suggestion is to allow the nerves, since trying to banish them only makes them worse. It's possible to be nervous and yet still be connected and alive when you sing. Concentrate on your imaginary circumstances, your preparation. Remember, the song is about your imaginary partner, not you.

Be careful how you use your time immediately preceding entering the audition room. What you do while you're waiting to go in will greatly affect what happens in your audition. Don't sit out there chatting with people. You can tell your friends "Excuse me, I need to be quiet and concentrate before I go in." Close your eyes and meditate a little by following your breath, or listen through headphones to a guided meditation tape. Engage yourself in positive, supportive self-talk or affirmations: "I deserve to have a great time in this audition—it's safe for me to have a great time—I choose to have a great time; I'm allowed to feel all of my emotions as I go through this audition, etc." Another technique that can be very helpful in launching your audition is to have the preparation for your song either written out or spoken on tape ("It's Friday afternoon and my boyfriend Jim just got home from a horrible experience at an audition…"), and then to either read or listen to it while you're waiting to go in.

Once you enter the room go about your business efficiently. You can give a friendly greeting from across the room to the auditors. There may be one person watching or a whole panel of producers, directors, etc. You can ask about that before you go in so that you're not thrown when you see them. Walk directly to the pianist and give him or her a few basic instructions. Here's the way I suggest you do that: Tell him or her the name of the song if it's not clearly written on the music. I've had the experience of being given a song to play with no title on it, and then four bars into it I realize it's a song I know and could have played better from the start had I known what song it was. Then give what I call the **Road map**—that is, where does it start and end, are there any cuts in the music or any repeats? Point out any surprises, like key changes or radical tempo changes so that the pianist can be prepared. Next give the **Tempo**. Unless the song is sung entirely "ad lib," or without a tempo, the pianist will need you to give a clear, steady beat. Usually I find it best to quietly sing a line of the song while gently tapping the beat on

> Sometimes I think people get too worked up trying to find the perfect song for this show, for this character. That can be a mistake, and they go in a direction that's not right for the character. Sometimes they don't represent themselves so well with that; they don't show who they are, and I think sometimes that's an important thing to get from somebody in an audition. I sort of feel like it's good to know what the raw materials are with somebody when you meet them in an audition.
>
> *Ted Sperling, Conductor/ Director/Orchestrator*

your own thigh. Don't snap in the pianist's face—they hate that. This whole process of giving directions to the pianist is important and should be practiced before the audition. Often people will throw their music in front of the accompanist, not say anything and then walk out to do their audition. That's a mistake for a couple of reasons. First of all it's rude and it alienates the pianist, which is a really bad idea—he or she is about to be your support system and performance partner, so make an ally of him or her. Second of all you'll not get the kind of playing you'll need if you don't clue them in about the road map and tempo. Be forewarned: accompanists can be rude and cantankerous themselves, and occasionally one may just wave you away as you begin to give them instructions, perhaps telling you they know the song. You really have no choice in that situation but to let it go and go ahead with the audition. If it's any comfort, know that they're treating all the other singers just as badly. One way to avoid all potential problems with the accompanist is to bring your own person with you. Some singers will only go in to auditions with their own pianist. The auditors will be impressed that you went to the trouble of hiring someone, and you won't have to be concerned with the in-house pianist's ability or attitude. Of course it can get expensive to do it that way, but for an audition that's important to you it may be worth it.

After you've given the pianist the road map and tempo, you can ask him or her to wait until you give them a nod before beginning to play. Then you walk to the middle of the room and take a moment to conjure up your imaginary world and your opening beat. A moment of silence will help the energy in the room to settle and make everyone focus on you;

it will increase anticipation and produce a sense that something important is about to happen. Manipulate the energy in the room in this way. Take a few seconds to enter another dimension, to create a relationship with your imaginary partner, then give the pianist a nod and be fully, emotionally alive in your imaginary world. If you're at a chorus audition, everything happens at warp speed, and there can be no "Please wait for me to nod." They'll most likely be playing your introduction as soon as you walk away from the piano. You'll get to sing 16 bars in most cases, and you'll have to move quickly through the process since they'll want to see as many people as they can.

If anything goes haywire during your audition—if the pianist plays at the wrong tempo, if you forget the lyrics, etc.—handle it calmly and with a sense of humor. If you don't make a big deal out of it neither will the auditors. Just regroup and start over or pick up from a convenient spot in the song.

After your audition try not to spend a lot of time second-guessing, trying to figure out what they thought of you. You'll never figure it out. Try to stay out of their heads and go instead to your own heart, get in touch with your own feelings. Support and comfort yourself, and if things went wrong, think about how you can improve your next audition. Having a career is a long road. Don't let a rock on the trail stop you from traveling forward.

When you get callbacks, sing the same material and wear the same clothes unless otherwise instructed. In this way they'll be able to remember you right away. It's a good idea to make notes in your appointment book about what you wear and sing.

> I'm moved by someone getting up there and communicating the truth, their truth, without asking to be loved in return in a certain way. Look at Mabel Mercer. A lot of people think Mabel Mercer was affected, but you listen to the best of her, and there's an archness there, but underneath that archness is such an incredible human connection. And that woman could hardly sing at all.
>
> *Stephen Holden, Critic*

Audition as often as you can, even for things you may not even be excited about. The more you do it the more relaxed you're likely to be about it. In addition, you never really know what you're auditioning for—one audition could lead to a part in an entirely different show. Even if you're not right for the show you're going in for, someone in the room might think of you for another project now or in the future. Bottom line: Always do your best. Make each audition an event and work with high stakes within your imaginary world. You can think of each audition as a performance you get to give. It can be fun, even with the nerves. Be alive in the room, alive in your work. Find the joy of performing. They'll love you if you're glad to be there. Walk in as if you're a winner—not arrogant but confident and upbeat.

And finally, find ways to stay alive creatively between auditions and jobs. Take classes and workshops, listen to recordings of singers and shows, sing for your friends, put together your own cabaret act. Be an artist in an ongoing way. Remember, the "product" you're selling is your ability to reveal yourself, to live truly and deeply in your performing.

Studying the Work of Masters

THERE IS MUCH TO BE LEARNED from the age-old tradition of studying the work of other artists in your field, masters who have gone before you and led the way. Let's take a look at some examples of performances that exemplify the kind of work I've discussed in this book. These can all be viewed on video. Rent them, study them, and let yourself be inspired by them.

The performer I most often point to as an example of someone who could act songs is Maria Callas. She was an operatic soprano who was unsurpassed in her ability to fully live on the musical stage. The arias she sang were extraordinarily difficult to execute, yet she sang them with musical integrity and at the same time acted them with spontaneity, clarity, and deep feeling. Her always-surprising and riveting musical phrasing and the intensity of the sound she made came out of her acting—her emotional involvement in the imaginary world of the piece. This was "real living under imaginary circumstances" of the highest order. She was a superb singing actress and a great, great artist. There's a video called "Dèbuts à Paris/The Paris Debut" filmed in 1958, on which she sings operatic arias in the first half of the concert, and the second act of "Tosca" in the second half. The whole tape is a feast with Callas bringing an intense inner life to bear on every phrase. She absolutely appears to be making it all up as she

> Well, Billie Holiday was one of the great naturals of all time. Nothing that came out of her mouth was ever untruthful. She had such a small range, and such a weird, funny little dry, sour voice. And yet what comes across is like sexual tragedy. She's damned, you know? It's the voice of someone who's damned. She's an animal. This lewd, longing, caterwauling, purring, seductive, primal animal. It's dangerous. Her voice and her life were one. There was just no camouflage.
>
> Stephen Holden, Critic

goes along. Watch her sing "Una voce poco fa" from "The Barber of Seville." It's fun to get an English translation and follow along as she sings in Italian, but even without knowing what the words mean, it's amazing to watch her work. First of all, she's as involved, specific, and interesting when she's not singing as when she is. She's listening to and incorporating into her experience every phrase that the orchestra plays. She's clearly in a specific place, talking and reacting to specific people. Her capacity to believe in her imaginary world is astonishing. And talk about reversals! You can't take your eyes away for a moment or you'll miss something unexpected and funny. You could not get anything else out of that aria. She justifies every note, every passage, every florid phrase as a human event. This is as good as it gets.

Rent the video of the television version of "Gypsy" starring Bette Midler for another great lesson. Her performance of "Rose's Turn" at the end of the story is magnificent. She walks out of her daughter's dressing room after their brutal confrontation—she's shattered and she rips into the spoken lines out there alone on-stage, then she moves spontaneously into the music. Her anguish and rage are genuine and deep, and she roars through the number, taking advantage of every musical element. It's a spellbinding, devastating performance.

There's a video called "Original Cast Album: Company" that chronicles the recording session of Stephen Sondheim's dazzling score for "Company." Get it and watch Dean Jones sing "Being Alive." I wish he didn't close his eyes so much, but even with that it's a model of connected singing. Then later you can see the brilliant Elaine Stritch battle it out with herself until she arrives at her remarkable performance of "The Ladies Who Lunch."

Robert Morse gives one of the funniest performances ever in "How to Succeed In Business Without Really Trying." Whether he's desperately mimicking Rudy Vallee in "Grand Old Ivy" or giving himself the ultimate pep talk in "I Believe In You," his work is like an amusement park ride, filled with organically-found audacity and diverse tactics.

As I said, study these and other recordings of great singing actors. Watching them work, seeing just how deeply engaged, really alive, specific and creative someone can be as they act a song will inspire you to take bigger risks in your own work. When you perform, let people see you at your most alive, your most powerful, your most needy, your most emotional, your most expressive.

Here's a quote from an interview in the New York Times with Barbara Cook, who was the premier Broadway leading lady of the late 1950s and who is today a superb cabaret performer:

"The one song that means the most to me (in my act) is

Rodgers' and Hart's 'He Was Too Good to Me.' I think of it as Mabel Mercer's song because the first time I heard it was when she sang it in the early '50s. It was around the time I was going to a lot of auditions where I would hear other singers whom I thought were technically superior to me. Somehow, remembering how Mabel sang that song helped me to realize that the only chance any singer has is to find out what is unique about yourself and get in touch with it. If you're able to be yourself, then you have no competition. All you have to do is try to get closer and closer to that essence."

Additional Thoughts

SOMETIMES YOU MAY WORK ON A SONG that activates a tremendous amount of emotion in you, and the feelings threaten your ability to keep singing. First of all, this is a wonderful problem—it's a huge asset to have access to your emotions in your work. There's an old saw that says an actor experiencing feelings on stage robs the audience of their feelings: "Don't you feel it, let them feel it!" That's definitely not my belief. I suggest that you allow and, in fact, welcome any feelings that organically occur in yourself as you work, with this proviso: No matter what you're feeling, pursue your objective. Remember, it's not about you, it's about your partner. If you allow your emotions to immobilize you, you're not doing your job. If you remain a warrior in the pursuit of your objective, then any feelings you experience along the way will only make your work that much more compelling and poignant. I often use as an example the scene in the movie "Kramer vs. Kramer" where Dustin Hoffman's young son falls off the jungle gym in the playground, cutting his head open. Hoffman rushes to him, scoops him up in his arms and races through the streets of New York to get him to an emergency room. He's extremely upset, full of emotion, but his objective is to get his boy to a doctor; he's not about to just sit down on the curb and cry. Get your job done, no matter how you're feeling.

> Don't copy. Be yourself. Don't try to be what you think other people are looking for. And find songs that you love to sing. I think things really start to work for an actor when they sing songs that they love to sing, and they're just themselves when they sing them.
>
> Jordan Thaler, Casting Director

I want to emphasize how important it is for you to be able to do the acting work I describe on your own, without the assistance of a director. You will seldom, if ever, get a director who either understands organic acting or has the time and desire to guide you into an emotionally-connected performance. It's necessary (and possible) for you to be able to do it yourself.

Most theatrical literature, whether plays, movie and television scripts, or songs, is written about situations that people abhor in real life; drama (including song) is not usually written about happy, healthy, well-adjusted characters. Conflict-free circumstances just aren't very interesting. Of course there are exceptions, but the majority of songs are written about people in trouble. We spend all of our time in our real lives trying to avoid exactly the situations that are depicted in songs. And yet if we're to truly act songs, truly live them in front of an audience, we need to be willing to visit those dark, painful places. If it's not an aching experience for you to sing "Send In the Clowns," or "This Nearly Was Mine," or "Lost In the Stars," you're not doing your job. Most people walk around pretending painful things aren't happening, pretending things don't hurt as badly as they do. But acting singers need to lean right into life's pain, to use it in their work. What a thing to ask! But what healing and wisdom and grace comes from working this way.

As a friend of mine who also coaches singers says, "Don't get caught singing." In other words, don't just make pretty sounds. Always sing with your primary concentration on the content of the lyrics. Think about what you're saying, to whom you're saying it, and what you hope to accomplish in your imaginary world by saying it. In this way you will reveal essential parts of yourself to your audience and this will interest them and move them. When you let your defenses down and allow an audience to watch you work from your heart, their hearts will be opened. You honor and serve them by letting them eavesdrop on you as you live, care, feel, strive and accomplish in your imaginary world.

Biographies

LYNN AHRENS, Lyricist/Librettist

Lynn Ahrens is the recipient of theater's triple crown—the Tony Award, Drama Desk Award and Outer Critics Circle Award, as well as two Grammy nominations, for the score of the Broadway musical *Ragtime* (based on the E.L. Doctorow novel) with long-time collaborator Stephen Flaherty and playwright Terrence McNally. Other notable theater credits include *Once On This Island* (London's Olivier Award for Best Musical), *Seussical*, based on the works of Dr. Seuss (2000 Grammy nomination, currently the number one most requested stock and amateur show in the U.S.), *Chita Rivera: The Dancer's Life*, *Dessa Rose*, *A Man of No Importance* (Outer Critics Circle Award for Best Musical and Best Score), *My Favorite Year*, *Lucky Stiff*, Madison Square Garden's *A Christmas Carol* (ten years in New York City). For film, she received two Academy Award nominations and two Golden Globe nominations for the songs and score of *Anastasia*, Twentieth Century Fox's first feature animation. She wrote the teleplay for A *Christmas Carol* (Hallmark Entertainment, starring Kelsey Grammer, NBC-TV.) Lynn received the Emmy Award and four Emmy nominations, and her songs are a mainstay of the renowned animated series *Schoolhouse Rock*.

pages 16, 45, 54, 58

MIKE BERNIKER, Record Producer

Mike Berniker is Vice President for A&R (Artists and Repertoire) Special Projects at Sony Music. He is legendary, having produced many major records in a vast array of categories, including Barbra Streisand's *People* and *The Barbra Streisand Album*, Eydie Gorme's *If He Walked Into My Life*, Johnny Mathis' *Mathis Sings Ellington*, Pete Seeger's *We Shall Overcome*, Jackie Mason's *Jackie Mason, Brand New*, the Broadway plays *The Real Thing* and *Ma Rainey's Black Bottom*, and the Broadway musicals *Nine*, *Dreamgirls*, *My One and Only*, *Side Show*, Cy Coleman's *Barnum*, *Sweet Charity*, *City of Angels*, *The Will Rogers Follies*, and *The Life*. This is just a small sampling of his work.

pages 1, 36, 51

JOSEPH CHURCH, Conducter/Composer/Arranger/Teacher

Joseph Church was the music director of *The Lion King* on Broadway for nine years. He also was music director of *The Who's Tommy* on Broadway and of *Randy Newman's Faust* at the Goodman Theatre in Chicago and the La Jolla Playhouse in San Diego. Joe was music director of the *Christmas Spectacular* at Radio City Music hall and of the national companies of *Little Shop of Horrors*. He has had long-standing involvements as a keyboard player and conductor with other Broadway shows, including *Les Miserables* and *Starlight Express*. As a composer, he has written incidental music for over thirty plays, and contributed arrangements and orchestrations to many other productions, on and off Broadway. His concert music includes the *Shainskiy Suite*, premiered in 2005 at Carnegie/Weil Hall. Joe holds a doctorate in composition from New York University, where he teaches composition, conducting, and musical theatre performance.

pages 10, 24, 31

SCOTT ELLIS, Director

Scott Ellis is one of the most respected and in-demand directors on Broadway. He moves back and forth between musicals and straight plays, and between new works and revivals. He has received Tony Award nominations for the Broadway productions of *Twelve Angry Men*, *She Loves Me*, *1776* and *Steel Pier*. Other Broadway productions include *The Boys From Syracuse*, *The Man Who Had All the Luck* with Chris O'Donnell, *The Rainmaker* with Woody Harrelson and Jayne Atkinson, *Picnic* (Outer Critics Circle nomination), *Company* (revival), and *A Month In the Country*. Off-Broadway Scott has directed *The Waverly Gallery*, *The Dog Problem*, *That Championship Season*, *Dark Rapture*, *And the World Goes 'Round: The Songs of Kander and Ebb* (Drama Desk, Outer Critics Circle Awards), and *Flora the Red Menace* (Drama Desk Nomination).

At the New York City Opera Scott has directed *110 in the Shade*, *A Little Night Music* with Jeremy Irons and Juliet Stevenson, also with Victor Garber, Judith Ivey and Zoe Caldwell at L.A. Opera. Her was the director and co-conceiver of *Sondheim: A Celebration at Carnegie Hall* and the Great Performances production *My Favorite Broadway: The Leading Ladies*.

pages 1, 8, 42

STEPHEN FLAHERTY, Composer

Stephen Flaherty is probably best know as the Tony Award-winning composer of the Broadway musical *Ragtime*. His other music for Broadway includes the scores for the musicals *Once On This Island*, *Seussical*, *My Favorite Year*, original songs for *Chita Rivera: The Dancer's Life* and incidental music for Neil Simon's *Proposals*. He is also the composer of the musicals *A Man Of No Importance* and *Dessa Rose*, both of which were produced by Lincoln Center Theater, the musical farce *Lucky Stiff* and *Loving Repeating: A Musical Of Gertrude Stein*, adapted from the works of Ms. Stein by Frank Galati. Steve's film work includes the song score for the animated feature *Anastasia*, for which he received two Academy Award nominations, Two Golden Globe nominations and a gold record for its soundtrack recording, which he co-produced. Among his numerous awards and honors are the Tony, Drama Desk, Outer Critics Circle, Los Angeles Critics Circle, and Olivier Awards and a citation from the National Academy of Arts and Letters, in addition to multiple nominations for the Oscar, Golden Globe and Grammy. Upcoming is *The Glorious Ones*, a new musical with Lynn Ahrens, Steve's collaborator for over twenty years.

pages 7, 13

DAVID FRIEDMAN, Composer/Lyricist/Musical Director

David Friedman's work has touched the lives of millions of people. He has written songs of inspiration, love, humor and hope (*Listen to My Heart*, *We Can Be Kind*, *Trust the Wind*, *My Simple Christmas Wish*, to name a few) that take on new emotional meaning in these challenging times. David starred, with five of New York's most gifted singer/actors, in a theatrical evening of his songs called *Listen to My Heart—The Songs of David Friedman*. He produced all of the late, great Nancy LaMott's CDs, and wrote many of Nancy's best-known songs. He has written a number of musicals, including *Chasing Nicolette*, *Desperate Measures*, and *King Island Christmas*. He conducted/vocal-arranged five shows on Broadway, as well as the Disney movie classics *Beauty and the Beast*, *Aladdin*, *Pocahontas*, and *Hunchback of Notre Dame*. He wrote music and lyrics for Disney's *Aladdin and the King of Thieves* and the sequel to *Bambi*. His songs have been recorded by Diana Ross, Barry Manilow, Petula Clark, Leslie Uggams, Jason Alexander, Kathie Lee Gifford, and Linda Eder, and many others. David recently published a songbook containing sixty-three of his best-known songs.

pages 1, 21, 62

STEPHEN HOLDEN, Critic

Stephen Holden is one of the leading cultural critics in America. He writes film and music reviews for the New York Times. Over the years he has reviewed all kinds of popular music, including rock, jazz, theater and cabaret. Stephen's writing is brilliant and trenchant, and a review from him puts a performer on the map. He has written many important "think pieces" for the Times about various artists and aspects of American culture.

pages 8, 18, 71, 76, 78

ROB MARSHALL, Director/Choreographer

Rob Marshall has had an amazing career, which took him from being a Broadway chorus dancer to being an A-list film director. He made his debut as a film director with the Academy Award-winning screen adaptation of the Kander and Ebb musical *Chicago*. Rob started out in New York performing in shows like *Cats* and *Zorba*. He quickly got jobs as Dance Captain and Assistant Choreographer, and was soon doing his own brilliant choreography for shows on Broadway such as *Victor/Victoria* and the revivals of *She Loves Me*, *Damn Yankees*, *Company* and *A Funny Thing Happened On the Way to the Forum*. He moved to television work, choreographing *Mrs. Santa Claus* starring Angela Lansbury, *Rodgers and Hammerstein's Cinderella*, and Tim Robbins' production of *The Cradle Will Rock*. Back on Broadway, Rob made his directorial debut by co-directing, with Sam Mendes, and choreographing the hit revival of *Cabaret*. That same year he directed the revival of *Little Me* starring Faith Prince and Martin Short. Rob's first directing job in television was the ABC adaptation of *Annie*, for which he won Emmys as director and choreographer, and which brought him to the attention of Harvey Weinstein, head of Miramax, leading to the *Chicago* film. Subsequently Rob directed the movie *Memoirs of a Geisha*.

pages 5, 11, 19, 69

TED SPERLING, Conductor/Orchestrator/Director

Ted Sperling is the most prominent Broadway music director of his generation. In 2005 he won the Tony and Drama Desk Award (with Adam Guettel and Bruce Coughlin) for his orchestrations of *The Light in the Piazza*, for which he was also music director. Other Broadway credits as music director/conductor/pianist include *Dirty Rotten Scoundrels, The Full Monty, How to Succeed in Business Without Really Trying, Kiss of the Spider Woman, Angels in America, My Favorite Year, Falsettos, Drood, Les Miserables, Roza,* and *Sunday in the Park With George.* Ted was also an original cast member of the Broadway musical *Titanic.* Off-Broadway credits as music director include *A Man of No Importance, Wise Guys, A New Brain, Saturn Returns, Floyd Collins, Falsettoland,* and *Romance in Hard Times.* As a stage director his work includes the world premieres of three musicals: *See What I Wanna See, Charlotte: Life? Or Theater?* and *Striking 12,* as well as a revival of *Lady in the Dark* starring Andrea Marcovicci. He has conducted the scores for the films *The Manchurian Candidate* and *Everything Is Illuminated,* and directed the short film, *Love Mom,* starring Tonya Pinkins, which has been shown in five international festivals. Ted has been soprano Audra McDonald's music director since 1999.

pages 42, 45, 65, 70, 73

JORDAN THALER, Casting Director

Jordan Thaler has been a casting director for over two decades, working in theater, film and television and has been working for over eighteen years at the Public Theater (New York Shakespeare Festival), casting over 150 productions Off-Broadway and at the Delacorte Theater in Central Park, including Shakespeare, new plays and musicals. On Broadway Jordan was the casting director for *Caroline, Or Change, Take Me Out* (Tony Award, Best Play 2003), *The Wild Party,*

Bring in 'Da Noise, Bring in 'Da Funk, On The Town and *The Tempest*. Jordan additionally works as both a teacher and guest lecturer at various university training programs for actors throughout the country.

pages 32, 82

JIM WILHELM, Agent

Jim Wilhelm is currently the president of Douglas, Gorman, Rothacker & Wilhelm, Inc. (DGRW), one of New York City's preeminent theatrical agencies since its formation in 1988. Over the years, Mr. Wilhelm has represented television and film actors such as Academy Award winner Olivia de Havilland, Dan Lauria, Lainie Kazan, Stephanie Zimbalist, Sharon Gless and Karen Valentine, daytime television stars Ron Raines, Catherine Hickland and Scott Holmes as well as Broadway stars Sandy Duncan, Douglas Sills, Alice Ripley, Karen Mason, Kathleen Chalfant, Andrea McArdle and Brian Stokes Mitchell. Jim has conducted seminars and master classes on auditioning and working in the theater at conservatories and universities across the country including NYU, North Carolina School of the Arts, Boston Conservatory and, most prominently, at the University of Cincinnati/ College Conservatory of music (CCM), where he established a scholarship fund in the name of his late client and friend, the Broadway and recording artist Laurie Beechman.

pages 25, 51

SUGGESTED READING:

The Artist's Way *by Julia Cameron*
Sanford Meisner On Acting
  by Sanford Meisner and Dennis Longwell
A Practical Handbook for the Actor
  by Melissa Bruder, et al
Respect for Acting *by Uta Hagen*
Audition *by Michael Shurtleff*
Acting, the First Six Lessons *by Richard Boleslavsky*
Story *by Robert McKee*
Poetics *by Aristotle*
Walking on Alligators *by Susan Shaughnessy*
The Drama of the Gifted Child *by Alice Miller*
Banished Knowledge *by Alice Miller*

About the author:

David Brunetti is a writer, musician, and teacher in New York City. He appeared on national television as the one-man "house band"/pianist on *The Vicky Lawrence Show* on FOX. He was also seen nationally on PBS in the documentary *Twitch and Shout*. His original music was heard off-Broadway in *Trophies* at the Cherry Lane Theater. He has served as vocal coach, musical director, and accompanist for Art Garfunkel, Judy Collins, Jennifer Holliday, Michael Feinstein, Eartha Kitt, Christopher Durang, Gregory Hines, Donna McKechnie, Nicol Williamson, Della Reese, Sam Harris, Marni Nixon, Leslie Uggams, Faith Prince, Donna Murphy, Paul Giamatti, Academy Award-winner Geena Davis, as well as for performers in almost every musical on Broadway. He has musical directed and played keyboards on and off-Broadway, in shows including *Blues In the Night* (Broadway, Off-Broadway, and London), *Nunsense*, *Forever Plaid*, *Les Miserables*, at the Roundabout and the Manhattan Theatre Club, and in most of the cabaret rooms in New York. He has taught master classes in New York, London, Sweden, Denmark, and at Florida State University. For further information, please visit www.actingsongs.com.

Printed in Great Britain
by Amazon